2BeCourageous

(Living with a Stranger)

2BeCourageous

(Living with a Stranger)

One family's open and raw account
living in a world of early-onset Alzheimer's
and Frontotemporal Dementia.

Heidi A. DeBoer

ELM HILL

A Division of
HarperCollins Christian Publishing

www.elmhillbooks.com

2BeCourageous
(Living with a Stranger)
One family's open and raw account
living in a world of early-onset Alzheimer's
and Frontotemporal Dementia.

Published in Nashville, Tennessee, by Elm Hill, an imprint of Thomas Nelson. Elm Hill and Thomas Nelson are registered trademarks of HarperCollins Christian Publishing, Inc.

Elm Hill titles may be purchased in bulk for educational, business, fund-raising, or sales promotional use. For information, please e-mail SpecialMarkets@ThomasNelson.com.

Scripture quotations marked ESV are from the ESV® Bible (The Holy Bible, English Standard Version®). Copyright © 2001 by Crossway, a publishing ministry of Good News Publishers. Used by permission. All rights reserved.

Scripture quotations marked KJV are from the King James Version. Public domain.

Scripture quotations marked NASB are from New American Standard Bible®. Copyright © 1960, 1962, 1963, 1968, 1971, 1972, 1973, 1975, 1977, 1995 by The Lockman Foundation. Used by permission. (www.Lockman.org)

Scripture quotations marked NIV are from the Holy Bible, New International Version®, NIV®. Copyright © 1973, 1978, 1984, 2011 by Biblica, Inc.® Used by permission of Zondervan. All rights reserved worldwide. www.Zondervan.com. The "NIV" and "New International Version" are trademarks registered in the United States Patent and Trademark Office by Biblica, Inc.®

Scripture quotations marked NKJV are from the New King James Version®. © 1982 by Thomas Nelson. Used by permission. All rights reserved.

Scripture quotations marked NLT are from the Holy Bible, New Living Translation. © 1996, 2004, 2007, 2013, 2015 by Tyndale House Foundation. Used by permission of Tyndale House Publishers, Inc., Carol Stream, Illinois 60188. All rights reserved.

Library of Congress Cataloging-in-Publication Data

Library of Congress Control Number: 2019906813

ISBN 978-1-400326662 (Paperback)
ISBN 978-1-400326679 (eBook)

CONTENTS

DEDICATION

This book is dedicated to my husband, Chet, the bravest person I have ever known, taking on his illness greatheartedly through the highs and the lows.

To my son, Jake, who stood by his dad and myself during the six-year struggle we endured, opting to live at home while in college so he could help and be with his dad.

To my daughter, Chesanne, for coming over several times a week to spend the day. She came and brought my grandchildren to give us some normalcy and distraction, to give and show her support, and to get me out of the house occasionally.

To my mom, Marge (93), for being on the other end of the phone whenever I needed to call her to vent, always offering a happy voice of encouragement and love. She passed on March 5th, 2018. She is greatly missed.

To my Facebook family and prayer warriors who stood by us with encouraging words and much prayer.

This book is based on one family's true story of their journey, caring for their loved one with dementia. When you have ten different people with dementia, you have ten different stories. This is ours.

Introduction

Definition of Courageous (Webster's Dictionary): "Very brave: having or showing courage."
Courageous Synonyms: "bold, brave, dauntless, fearless, gallant, great-hearted, gutsy, heroic, valiant."

2BeCourageous

" I, Heidi, take you, Chet, for better and for worse, in sickness and health, for richer and poorer, through trials and tribulations."

"I, Chet, take you, Heidi … " and they lived happily ever after. That's how it is supposed to end. This book is just a small part of our many stories.

"2BeCourageous" has many meanings to different people. To be diagnosed with any type of dementia, or becoming a caregiver to a loved one with dementia twenty-four-seven is 2BeCourageous. Though most caregivers and patients go unrecognized for their gallant efforts to live with or care for a person with dementia, these people are true heroes and should not be forgotten and lost in the madness that surrounds them. This is now their new normal.

2BeCourageous first started out as a blog on WordPress, and then I moved it to a blog on Facebook. Much of this book is formatted from posts written by me from my blog/journal and my personal page, from our day-to-day lives dealing with dementia. I will share what I have learned and my many mistakes. I'm not an expert or a doctor, I'm just a real-life person who lived it. However, after six years living in the Alzheimer's World day and night, I wish to share what I have learned. It will be brutally raw, no holding back. If nothing else, I'm hoping you'll be able to relate to our story and not feel so alone in your own journey. We are a Christian family that can go through a high range of emotions and, even on the best of days, we can fall short and end up not following the rules. Yes, there are rules to follow. Christ has rules for daily life, and, when it comes to people with dementia, there are rules we try to live by, for instance:

1 – Do not argue with the person with dementia.
2 – Live in their world; they no longer live in our world.
3 – Divert their attention elsewhere when they insist on something we know is wrong.
4 – Do not argue with the person with dementia.
5 – Don't ask if they remember this or that.
6 – If they forget they asked something, and ask over and over, go with it. Just tell them the answer or divert their attention.
7 – Did I say don't argue with the person with dementia? Ha! This was the hardest rule for me. You will see that I wasn't good at it.

I hope you can relate and maybe learn from our experiences and mistakes. I talk a lot about God because He is front and center in our lives. I am a Christian, and I mess up. No one is perfect, but if you keep God as your focus, you will make it through your journeys. The Bible verses that I've included gave me encouragement when I thought I couldn't go on. Some taught me lessons about myself and my family.

I get very personal and talk about things that most people hide and keep quiet about; sugarcoating dementia only hides the truths of the disease. Follow us on our journey. We hope you will take away from it what benefits you the most.

DANCING IN THE RAIN

Figure 1 Chet and Heidi DeBoer

I will throw away my red umbrella,

and, with you, go barefoot in this rain.

We'll dance our way through all the new storms

and put aside this heartfelt pain.

Our life from here on out should be adventurous,

jumping from planes or bungee off a bridge.

Well, at least jumping in mud puddles, you and me together.

We will praise our Lord our God for the old and new memories,

that in our hearts we shall cherish and keep forever.

2BeCourageous hand in hand, I Love You!

HEIDI DEBOER 2012 ©

"You will keep him in perfect peace whose mind is stayed on You because he trusts in You."

ISAIAH 26:3 NKJV

CHAPTER 1

THE DIAGNOSIS

It was November 2012, and, as I sat in the neurologist's office in Nashville, TN on our third visit within a year, I watched my husband, Chet, stare straight ahead. No expression on his face, just waiting in silence for the doctor. When the doctor came in, he started the usual round of tests.

Chet is the man I fell forever in love with after placing an ad in the *Michigan Single File Magazine*. I was looking for a loving Christian man, one who was outgoing, self-reliant, a hard worker, and he had to be a cowboy who loved horses and dogs and wanted a couple of kids! I explained I was a little bit country and a little bit rock and roll. I had worked at two horse farms and was, at that time, self-employed in a craft business and cleaning business. I had long golden hair and a fun-loving sense of humor and was serious about the type of man I was looking to meet. After receiving several odd letters from men with whom I had nothing in common and did not interest me, Chet's letter arrived.

He sent photos of himself with his horses and the cutest black German shepherd puppy ever along with a Siberian Husky, whose names were Willard and Harold. Chet explained in his letter that he had just started his own business as a store consultant doing interior store layouts and fixture designs for Christian bookstores around the country. He previously spent sixteen years doing the same for a large Christian bookstore chain.

Chet was a cowboy at heart with a small horse farm and a love for animals and children. We met for the first time at Cheddars on January 9th, 1991. He was wearing cowboy boots, a cowboy hat, an Australian Drover coat that went to his ankles, and, of course, a Western shirt and jeans. His eyes sparkled and he had a great goatee. His smile melted my heart and we had so much in common, even knowing many of the same people. After dinner, feeling very smitten, I went home and told my mom that he was the one I would marry … and he was!

Chet proposed, singing a rap song (so out of character, it was adorable) on February 22nd, 1991. Then, on July 20th, 1991, six months after the month we met and both in our thirties, Chet (37) and I (34) married, having a country Western dream wedding.

We had that relationship where you knew what the other was thinking, and we wanted and liked so many of the same things. I had surprised Chet with a painting of a foal painted by an artist who was a friend of his for our wedding. Chet surprised me and bought me a real horse, a beautiful buckskin mare, for my wedding gift.

I attribute the story of our meeting as being one of God's doings. Chet's experience with women was that he had been treated like a brother or handed the friend card; he was an all-around nice guy. One day, very overwhelmed and frustrated with how his life was going, Chet broke down and cried and prayed to God to please bring him someone to love. I don't know how long after that when he saw my ad, but Chet never bought or ordered that singles' magazine. It had shown up in his mailbox with a label that said, "Complimentary Copy!" We still have it. I believe God wanted us together. Chet told me the book fell open to the page I was on; he said it sounded too good to be true.

Chet was the president of the Grand Rapids Western Horse Club, and we were active with this great group of people. Gathering for potluck dinners, going on trips to barn dances, and going on hay rides were just a few of the club's activities. We had six horses and enjoyed breeding and raising the babies. Watching the miracle of birth never got old; our life seemed perfect.

I kept my cleaning clients and dropped the craft shows at this time. We lived in a unique two-bedroom home that Chet had built. It was called a berm home, where the dirt surrounds the house up to the windows. We lived on ten acres, and it was our little paradise hidden from the street by the trees. We named it Honey Creek Farms.

Three years into our marriage, we had beautiful twins—a boy named Jake and a girl named Chesanne—in July of 1994. They, too, have a story. We conceived them through infertility procedures after trying unsuccessfully since our wedding to have children. We went through ups and downs … wanting children and not being successful. I had the GIFT procedure done, where my eggs (5) and Chet's donations were put near the fallopian tubes; it was to happen naturally from there. A day later, the doctor called and said that he had placed some of the sperm with the ten additional eggs that we were going to freeze. The sperm would not go near the eggs. That meant the procedure I had done most likely wouldn't work. I was devastated and I cried and cried. Chet couldn't comfort me. The next day, the doctor called back and he said that, for the first time in their hospital (it had been done elsewhere), they tried the ICSI procedure where they injected one sperm into each egg. Two eggs survived the fertilization and the doctors put them into my uterus. That was another "God thing," or miracle, as I like to call it. The doctors did not charge us for that second procedure. Both eggs "took" and became my twins. I was overjoyed, I finally was going to be a mom!

I was considered high risk due to my age and had to see the doctor more often. I had an unremarkable pregnancy; nothing happened out of the norm. I threw Chet a birthday/baby shower combination and called it a "First-Time Dad at 40" party. Family and friends came to celebrate with us with gifts for the twins.

The twins' arrival came two weeks early. My water broke on July 19th at 6:00 a.m. and, of course, I was in a panic. We hurried off to the hospital. My mom and dad were in the delivery room with us and got to watch the birth. My dad wouldn't look; he just focused on a corner in the room and looked like he was going to pass out. Looking back, we laughed at the memory! I was not laughing during labor, though, and Chet kept telling me to focus on the baby horse picture we put on the wall. I yelled, "I can't see it! You focus on it, leave me alone!" The memory still makes me smile.

Jacob Avery came shooting out like a football at 2:08 and the doctor almost dropped him. Chesanne Daly took her sweet time coming out, and waited thirty minutes after Jake arrived to show up at 2:38. The twins had to stay in the NICU for fourteen days because Chessie ran a fever when she was born, and I tested positive for the Strep B. Jake was just a little underdeveloped, so they kept him too. My parents and Chet's dad all came to take turns holding the babies. (Chet's mom passed away from cancer surgery complications one month before I met him, so I never got to meet her.) The day finally came when we could take the twins home. We were so excited … and nervous at the same time!

It was a happy time and my mom often came and helped to take care of the twins. Chet would travel for his work and Mom would stay with me. I was so blessed to have Chet work from a home office when he wasn't traveling. He was a hands-on dad and got to experience all the twins' milestones as they happened.

Chet was my shining light, always keeping God first. His faith was unstoppable and his family was always a top priority, even over work. I felt so secure in that! I felt nothing could go wrong.

"Humble yourselves, therefore, under the mighty hand of God so that at the proper time he may exalt you, casting all your anxieties on him, because he cares for you."

1 PETER 5:6–7 ESV

CHAPTER 2

LOSS OF HOME AND MIND

B ack in the neurologist office, the doctor brought my attention back to what was happening in the room. My mind went off into a silent panic attack while my heart was falling to the bottom of my stomach. The doctor just gave Chet another good thirty plus minutes neurological memory exam. It had math, spelling, drawing clocks, presidents, dates, hand movements … and nothing was clicking for him. I wanted so badly to answer for him! *This is not happening!* I thought. But Chet did come up with one president finally, and leave it to a Democratic President to catch Chet's memory, but he couldn't come up with his name, so he said to the doctor, "Oh, you know! That guy who had all that sex while in office!" This broke the tension in the room, and we all laughed. Then there was dead silence as the doctor wrote and thought things out. I so hated the silence.

The doctor stepped out of the room and my thoughts then wandered off to May 1995, when we went through a pesticide poisoning by a local pesticide company inside our berm home. The poisoning was confirmed through testing by the Department of Agriculture because we, including our nine-month-old twins and the cat, all became very sick. The company was found at fault and fined and was ordered to clean up the crawl space, the entire house, and the attic. Pesticides were found on the baby cribs and toys and in all of the air vents. This was due to a dust sprayed in the furnace plenum, which was our home's crawl space. The cleanup went a foul when black mold formed due to water left in the plenum crawl space. The company had sprayed the water in with a garden hose where it settled between torn plastic and wood beams, and never dried out. The mold was discovered by additional testing a year later because of continued illnesses with the whole family. We were so worried about the long-term effects of the mold and poisons, it added to the behind-the-scenes stress.

The house was condemned by the Health Department, something that probably wouldn't happen today due to improved professional cleanup techniques. We sued; our dream home that Chet had built was no longer livable. We bought a thirty-foot camping trailer to live in on the property. We lived in it for fifteen months through a Michigan winter, and, the next summer, moved it to a resort camping/mobile home park. We had to let the house go to the bank.

We eventually rented a townhouse and tried to get some normalcy back. We sold our horses and had to put down Harold, our German shepherd, due to paralysis. We gave our other dog to Chet's brother who had thirty-five acres to run on. We kept the camper for weekend getaways. To this day, if you ask my family, they would tell you that the best times were living in the camper. I felt safe in it while I no longer felt safe in my home.

****

The doctor came back in the room and started to apologize to us as we both sat there nervously. You know that's never a good thing when the doctor starts out with, "I'm so sorry." He told us he needed to change Chet's original diagnosis of "pseudo (meaning false) dementia" that he made at the end of 2011. The doctor had felt that Chet's symptoms were caused by depression and stress and were said to be curable. Unfortunately, Chet did not respond to any of the treatments (antidepressants) for it and was getting worse. The doctor said he believed his new diagnosis to be early-onset Alzheimer's (professionally written out as dementia, probably of the Alzheimer's type), but he didn't want to make that call. He told us, speaking in his heavy Middle Eastern accent, "This is not curable, there is no treatment to slow it down, just medication to help with symptoms." He briefly mentioned FTD (Frontotemporal Dementia) but was unsure since dementia was not his specialty. He referred us to a neurologist specializing in Alzheimer's and other types of dementias. He requested this new doctor to have more evaluations and memory testing done to confirm or contradict this diagnosis of early-onset Alzheimer's. The doctor apologized again and said, "I hope I am wrong."

I thought, *He hoped? Not more than Chet and I both did, surely!*

Walking to the car, Chet said nothing at all. I started sweating and shaking, having a mild anxiety attack. I had tears in my eyes that I fought and kept wiping away. We needed a concrete diagnosis if Chet were to go on disability, but this? I couldn't talk; I had all I could do just to keep calm and drive home.

On the ride home, my mind kept traveling back to the pesticides; the thoughts haunt me to this day. I wonder if they caused this in my husband or somehow triggered it. He struggled with memory shortly after it happened, but we would tease him about it for it was just little things he would forget, and we would blow it off. He also developed diabetes shortly after the poisoning with sudden weight loss. Blood sugar levels that are off can affect thinking also.

We had won a small settlement in court, but not enough to cover the house and all the testing and lawyer expenses. It was such a stressful ordeal, and we were made to look like money hungry people making up our illnesses even when we had medical evidence to show how sick we all had been. We opted out of any appeals process and just moved on with our lives; that was healthiest for all of us. I couldn't live with the stresses of the legal process any longer; it can be a joke.

I had developed fibromyalgia, a chronic pain disease, after the poisoning. I was diagnosed in 1996 and have lived with chronic pain ever since. The twins had their battles with our daughter having respiratory problems and bloody noses, a couple of hospitalizations, and several trips to ER as a toddler. Our son began getting migraines with vomiting starting at three years old; he was hospitalized for them at age seven. We all seemed to end up with something wrong with us, and it will always stay in the back of my mind that the poisoning may have been the cause.

I was the fixer of the family. Chet would call me "Doctor Mom" when one of them got sick, or an animal was sick or hurt. I was right there doctoring them. But I felt helpless now, I didn't know how to fix this. Even all the praying to God didn't fix my husband. Perhaps the doctors are wrong, but my gut feeling says differently.

After living in the townhouse for two years, and life returning to normal, we decided to buy a double-wide home. We put it on the lakefront in the park where we camped in Gowen, Michigan and we sold the camper.

My father passed away unexpectedly in 2003 and I took it very hard. I had so much I needed to tell him. The following year, we moved my mother and my sister up to the lake in their own home that we could see from our house. I was so excited to have them near me.

During the time at the townhouse, I had started a magnetic jewelry company making magnetic beaded jewelry that helped people with inflammation and pain. It was a huge success and, by the time we moved to the lake, we were up to forty arts and crafts shows a year. Chet started helping me and man, was he a good designer of jewelry! My mom also helped design and make jewelry; she rocked it also! We filled a 10×10 show tent with the product. The kids would travel with us to big shows where we would stay the night, and they got involved working the tent also.

There were always activities for the kids and adults at the park we lived in all summer long: dances, karaoke, movie nights, golf cart poker, five playgrounds, a lake, and a beach. There were campfires and lots of friends. Life was good. We got our happy back!

"And we boast in the hope of the glory of God. Not only so, but we also glory in our sufferings, because we know that suffering produces perseverance; perseverance, character; and character, hope. And hope does not put us to shame because God's love has been poured out into our hearts through the Holy Spirit, who has been given to us."

ROMANS 1:2–5 NIV

CHAPTER 3

SYMPTOMS AND LIFE-CHANGERS

In hindsight, Chet's symptoms did not just happen overnight. This crept in our back door and lived with us for years. Plus, we just had so many stressors going on in our lives at once for such a long period. At first, it seemed pseudodementia made sense, looking at all Chet had to cope with, all that went on and was put on him. Losing the house he had built, and the poisoning was a huge stressor. We didn't know what the poison could do to us long-term.

In 2006, things took a turn and for the worse. Chet's business had been hurting. Small mom-and-pop Christian bookstores were being run out by the big box stores and modern electronic book readers. They just couldn't compete, and the small stores were Chet's bread and butter. My jewelry craft business and Chet's business suffered greatly by 2006, with Chet's business having two contracts drop out that spring due to financial problems of their own. One contract was especially difficult as our money and time had already been put into it, and the store had not paid Chet for the work he had done to date.

After five years of success doing arts and craft shows, Michigan's downward economy was affecting my jewelry business. That sixth and seventh year fell drastically in sales and, at some shows, I barely made booth fees. Other vendors were suffering also, some not making anything. I saw no way to save it. I had competition from people buying pre-made magnetic jewelry from China and saying they made it to get into shows. They sold it for cheap. I couldn't compete. We fell behind on bills, and the calls started.

Creditors were making us look like evil people of the earth, calling us names and swearing at us. Creditors even called my mother, and were mean to her too, even though she had nothing to do with our debt. I would cry after each phone call, and we got several a day. We stopped answering the phone, but it would ring and ring and nasty messages were left on the machine. They did not care that harassing phone calls are illegal. That did not stop those horrible people.

I could not cope with the calls anymore I felt devastated inside; I had a breakdown in May of 2006 and wanted to kill myself. I thought my life insurance would pay Chet, which would stop all the creditors from calling and being mean to us. I spent thirty-two days in a hospital after taking my husband's gun and running away, threatening to kill myself with it. Somehow in my mind, it made sense to give myself up to stop the madness of the calls. That summer, I ended up going doctor to doctor, in and out of facilities, with each one adding more medication on to me. I didn't know if I was coming or going. Chet was amazing through this whole ordeal, standing by me and helping me through this very hard time. His love for me was nonstop. I adored him and felt guilty for even thinking about killing myself.

In November of 2006, Chet was offered a job in Tennessee with one of his competitors in his field of Christian bookstore design and installations. He moved the family within a month's time in late December 2006. I was not happy; I didn't want to move away from my mom or our home. We had just moved my mom and sister to the park on the lake where we lived, so we could be close to each other.

Well, we settled in La Vergne, TN, and the kids did well acclimating to the new school and area. They were in the seventh grade. We started at a new church and made new friends, and the kids started attending youth group at church. We all went to family camp through the church and it was a blast.

I had a few rough spots with depression and my new doctor here took me off some of the medications, feeling it was way too much. I felt alive again and life was looking up. I felt that I could finally relax … until life took yet another turn.

Chet lost his new job in August of 2008 due to a lack of work for him to do. The company was also hurting and couldn't support his services any longer. He was on unemployment for over a year and didn't have any luck finding a job in his field or pay scale. He took a part-time job at a home goods store.

Chet's father passed in October 2010 from prostate cancer and that had a big effect on Chet. We drove home to Michigan but didn't make it in time for him to say goodbye to his dad.

Chet had so much stress on him that it looked like pseudodementia to the doctors, but, at the same time, my intuition said, "No, that's not the answer." I knew my husband and deep down I feared what was wrong with him was Alzheimer's. I researched it over and over and I wouldn't stop until he was diagnosed correctly; but, at the same time, he was too young to have it, I thought. After all, I thought Alzheimer's was a disease of the elderly. I never heard of early-onset.

I weaned off most my medications that I was on but still suffered depression that I was slowly overcoming with setbacks and another hospitalization in 2010. I received electric shock therapy that I have no memory agreeing to. The shock treatments wiped my memory of about a month or more, which I find out is normal. I didn't want to admit it but the treatment helped me a lot.

We still had the evil creditors trying to find us. We had new numbers, but they were harassing my mom and she had to change her phone number. We filed for bankruptcy in 2011 and that stopped the calls. I felt lower than low having to file but we had no choice.

We had to wait several months for the new appointment with a new neurologist and still no concrete answers. With no MRI images to look at yet, we got another diagnosis of pseudodementia with a promise of a cure. I was furious this doctor told my husband there was nothing to worry about and he could be cured. He blew us off, I felt! I thought, *How dare you to give him false hope! Chet already didn't feel he had anything wrong with him!* They had to calm me down and told me I should feel good about this.

I wasn't the only one upset by this. The false dementia diagnosis also irritated Chet's primary care doctor to no end. He said it was so obvious to him that it was Alzheimer's, so he wanted to start Chet on Aricept if they had it on hand, or they would get samples. I felt we were finally doing something for him.

We were given a follow-up appointment for more testing at the hospital. After the MRI was done, a team of residents in the Resident Neurology Clinic at Vanderbilt Medical Center (a teaching hospital) would see him next. New doctors meant new memory testing, and I felt better that they were still trying to diagnose Chet.

If you have sat through a loved one's memory testing, you will relate to what I did while my husband's tests were being administered. It became a game with me, hoping I wasn't getting dementia! I answered along in my head. It went something like this:

The doctor asked Chet, "What is today's date?"

My husband looked blankly at the doctor but, in my head, I said, *January 10ᵗʰ,"* Ha! One for me; I got it right!

Then the doctor asked, "What state are we in?"

I silently answered, *Tennessee.* Chet, after a long pause, said Tennessee, also. We both got it right!

The doctor then asked him, "Who is the President of the United States?"

I yelled out in my head, *Barack Obama!*

Chet said, "Oh, that idiot!"

Yes! We were both right again! (Just joking!) Then the doctor asked him his birth date. He could not answer. I could in my mind, though. His and my date.

Next, the doctor moved onto math. Great, not my strong suit, and I already knew Chet would have trouble. The doctor asked him, "Multiply 16×35?"

In my head, I responded, *What? Is that even fair? I need paper; I can't do this!* Chet couldn't either, which didn't make me feel better that I couldn't. He used to be a math whiz.

"Let's try another," said the doctor. "Count backward from 75 by 7s."

Me: *What? She is setting me up to fail…! I mean, my husband…. Yeah.*

I'm betting I'm not the only one who takes these exams for themselves, quietly in their heads, as the tests are being administered to loved ones. I think our fear intensifies over getting dementia ourselves after our loved ones are diagnosed because we thought these dearly loved people were invincible. Not in my wildest dreams or fears did I think my husband would be where he was now, with me now the head of the house, having to run the show.

I was so fearful of getting this disease, and nothing could happen to me. I needed to be here, together, calm, not showing fear, so that I could care for him. I was now his full-time caregiver. My kids needed me too! They were young adults now, seventeen, but this wasn't easy on them either, and it was up to me now to be invincible.

We were at that neurologists visit about forty-five minutes to an hour. We did these tests with every new neurologist and on every follow-up visit. Her math questions were not the norm, by the way, and more difficult than others in the past.

Chet drew the circle for the clock test in an actual circle this time instead of all distorted, and put all the numbers on it starting with twelve and going backward. I was in praise of this for he had never done this so correctly since his first test in 2011. I kept saying excitedly out loud, "He's never done this before. This is the first time he is on track! That's good, right?!" I got that sudden false hope this wicked disease threw at you every so often, just to break your heart again in the next moment. His response to "place the hands on the clock at 10 past 11" was to place his actual hand on the paper and look confused. So, the doctor told him again to "draw the clock hands at 10 minutes past 11" and Chet said, "I don't understand," and that elation I'd had suddenly stopped.

Chet's MRI came back looking like the brain of a very elderly person with dementia, with obvious gray matter shrinkage showing. The neurology residents told me they had never before seen this in their training with someone younger as Chet was, and it explained a lot of Chet's symptoms. They seemed quite startled by it and told me this was very serious! They referred Chet to another specialist in Vanderbilt who deals with dementia. After I refused to see the previous doctor who had promised a cure, they reassured me it was not pseudodementia. They explained the other doctors had not seen the MRI beforehand, and it's a hard diagnosis to make. Okay, I gave them that.

The man whose mind I used to be able to read said nothing that day. I no longer knew his thoughts, and his words no longer came out in the order he wished them to. Chet's loving support for us and his charming, loving ways I now yearned for. He had just turned fifty-eight.

The team of resident neurologists felt it looked like early-onset Alzheimer's (EOA). It had been a two-year battle for a diagnosis of EOA, but, when told to us again, my heart sank once more. Even though my intuition recognized it the whole time, it crushed me to hear it from these doctors. The tears came on quickly.

I now accepted the challenge and role of being the rock to keep the house from falling, and to keep God in front of us first. I accepted the role of helping the man who gave all of himself to his family to have some sense of dignity and self-worth and to feel loved. I was his voice, his care-giver, and his wife, and I knew I couldn't do this alone. I had days I fell short in patience and kindness. I prayed to God that He would give me wisdom and the ability to handle what was yet to come. I prayed that my depression would stay away and that the Holy Spirit's light would shine through me and guide me.

We were slowly starting to see changes in Chet in 2010. Memory lapses and a feeling that he was just tired and out of it at times. It was more than losing the keys or forgetting what day it was. These things were happening way too often. When we went home to Michigan for his dad's funeral, his sisters saw a big difference in him that I guess we were accustomed to being so close to him daily.

I've learned Alzheimer's and other dementias are not part of the natural aging process. In fact, younger and younger people are getting it. People who never had any symptoms or memory loss have been found to have the plaques and tangles of Alzheimer's in their brain upon autopsy, so there must be another factor that triggers the symptoms of dementia. If only they could figure it out! To me, that says the tangles and plaques could be forming in those early years before symptoms arrive. I have learned, according to the Alzheimer's Association, there are over 5.8 million people in the United States that are living with Alzheimer's. By 2050, it is projected to rise to 14 million. I thought, *How could Chet have Alzheimer's? He is too young!* I didn't know younger onset existed. I thought it was a geriatric disease.

I remember sitting at our desk in the living room in 2011 and Chet came out of the bedroom very frustrated. He threw down the checkbook, bill book, and bills on the desk in front of me. He said angrily, "Here, you do this from now on, I can't do it anymore!" and he walked away. Chet had always paid all the bills and taken care of the check book throughout our marriage; I wanted nothing to do with managing the money, so I was shocked and angry that he decided to throw it on me the way he did.

After looking at the bills and checkbook ledger, I had trouble reading what he wrote, his handwriting had gone downhill, and I found some of his figuring unfinished and wrong. I didn't understand what was going on at that point. I was at a loss. Then it came out; he told me a week later that he couldn't do the numbers anymore. I asked, "What do you mean you can't do the numbers anymore? That you don't want too?"

He said, "No, I can't do the math, I can't figure out the numbers. They make no sense." Then I knew we had a problem more serious than memory alone. He was also displaying a problem with his words, saying words opposite of what he meant and lost his math skills.

Chet took a part-time job at a home goods store after being on unemployment for over a year or more and not finding anything equivalent to his past jobs in pay or type of work. I remember him complaining that the managers would pick on him and speak rudely in telling him how to do his job. I found out later that it was because they had to remind him often what to do. He couldn't remember and, of course, it didn't make him look good. But he felt he was fine and doing a great job. He felt everyone was against him there.

Chet would go on job interviews and come back so frustrated because he couldn't remember what to say to questions he was asked. His words also betrayed him, coming out in the wrong order at times. In the fall of 2010, Chet took a new job full-time at a high school as a custodian. This job became the job from hell for him. He kept it for two years, but it was hard on him and he refused to reveal he was having problems with memory. He felt they didn't need to know. He wouldn't allow me to tell them.

"Children are a gift from the LORD; they are a reward from him."

PSALM 127:3 NLT

CHAPTER 4

LATE-NIGHT SURPRISES

To add to our house of stress in early 2011, this happened next which would change us all in one way or another.

Pretty much a normal day, kids were home after school, playing that odd machine controlled by thumbs where they stare into the TV. I'm on the computer and Chet headed to bed early, tired from a long day at work. Chessie's boyfriend, Brandon, was here for a while, and some of Chessie's friends were at the door and they all went outside. This is done when mom is not allowed to hear the conversation. I hate that! Then it was quiet. Quiet is nice.

Everyone left and Chessie, sixteen at this time came to me and said, "Mom, I have something I need to tell you."

I was very focused on the computer; the focus immediately broke, and I got a chill. I turned towards her and her face was buried in a pillow. I said jokingly, "You're pregnant?"

She said, "Yes."

My quick, brilliant response back was, "No you're not!"

"Mom, I took a test," she said. So, we dug out the test from the trash, and, sure enough, she bought one that spelled it out—"PREGNANT."

I said, "Maybe they forgot to put the 'NOT' in this one!" Yeah, nothing like humor to lighten the moment when your daughter tells you she just changed her life forever. We walked back out into the living room and I looked at her; there were so many things to say running through my mind, I couldn't keep up with them all, and only one thing seemed right. I hugged her, and I told her how much I loved her, and I told her I would support her and her baby.

I asked some questions in a calm, controlled voice (which shows the medications I'm on were working), then we went and told her brother. Jake swore he would be there for her and pound to the ground anyone who said anything bad about her. That's my boy!

Now, to wake her dad who does not wake easily and doesn't understand conversations until morning. I was not going to worry alone all night, so he was getting up! I made him sit up and talk to me, so I knew he was awake, then I told him. He was silent. He got up and made coffee. Said nothing for a long time. Then Chessie approached him for a hug, and he hugged her and told her he loved her. Then he went back to bed. No emotion, nothing, just made coffee and hugged her and said he loved her. Later, I hid in the garage and cried alone, so worried and afraid for her.

Her boyfriend, Brandon (18), loves her very much, and they have dated fifteen months. He wanted to marry her; she wanted to finish high school and maybe cosmetology school and see where that would bring them then. We agreed with that. They both wanted the baby even being so young. I knew there were those who thought adoption or even abortion was the only answer but, for our kids and this family, it was not. And I believe his family felt the same. It's a little soon for too many plans, so we prayed for wisdom from God that decisions were well-thought-out and prayed on together.

If I said I wasn't expecting "I'm expecting," I'd be lying. I played out the moment in my mind a few times. Does that mean I had no trust in them? I did! I believed, well, I kind of believed they wouldn't go there.

I can kind of believe my children but I can't kind of believe in God; you either do or you don't. I do, I also believe He has well-placed plans mapped out for my family; I'm sure I got the wrong map, but I am accepting it but will still pray for directions!

Teens, their hormones are raging. What does that even mean? They have mad hormones? No, I know, it's an excuse that's used for lack of self-control, something we can blame the poor choices they have made on. They made a choice!

But it won't happen to this family; we have it covered—the in-school sex classes, the home talks, the home lectures. The prayers to cover it. Church and youth group. Nope, not going to happen; we are covered, we are Christians! Oh, does that sound snooty or what? Very much so, it was meant to be. But that's how some people think. That's how we are looked upon by some people. They are Christian, so they are hypocrites; they just sinned. Christians sin, folks.

We are a Christian family that has its fair share of sin; we live in a world of sin, we also love and forgive our own and our neighbors. Family takes care of family even on the days we don't get along. As much as we were sitting here going, "Really? Did this just happen?" All the what-did-I-do-wrongs and should-have-done are meaningless now. It no longer mattered; at this point, there were two kids, scared, who need more love than ever before, more hugs than ever before, more family time than ever before. They needed to know they were okay. They needed to know we cared about them and their baby. What would one critical word justify? They knew they messed up. What was done was done.

We broke the news to Brandon's mom the next day because Brandon was too nervous to tell his parents. When we went to leave, his mom gave Chessie a hug and told her, "Everything will be all right; we'll get through this."

I told my daughter on Sunday, "Chessie, no matter what, you need to be proud of your baby. It's one of God's miracles, it is a gift, so you be proud and don't let anyone tell you differently because people will try to make it bad!"

That night, she posted the weekly baby chart on Facebook on the progress of her baby, which told everyone on her Facebook list she was pregnant. When you're not sure, you hold on and love them! ♥ Even when you are sure, hold on to them and love them.

So, on December 12, 2011, our grandson, Braydon Michael, was born. Brandon's mom and I were in the delivery room and watched our grandson be born. Our gift from God because we needed that little boy in our lives and his timing was good.

I'm not condoning teen sex before marriage; I believe they should wait. Yes, they shouldn't have had sex but don't take that wrong out on a baby. When God gives you such a gift, it's never a mistake—it's a child.

"My help comes from the Lord, the Maker of heaven and earth."

PSALM 121:2 NIV

CHAPTER 5

START OF JOURNAL

In the posts to follow, some post topics were mentioned in Chapter 1, the following posts from my blog-journal go into more detail. This was our day-to-day walk on this journey.

Blog Posts from 2BeCourageous on Facebook

2BeCourageous updated their status.
November 06, 2012 – 4:39 a.m.
My husband and I were talking about his main job the other day. He also works at the church doing custodial work part time.

By the second year, he hated the school job, mainly because he felt slighted and picked on and disliked what he was assigned to do. If poop was spread all over the boy's bathroom, it was Chet assigned to clean it. When the kids would stuff the toilets and overfill them, it was Chet who was assigned to clean it. Always him, he felt.

I talked to him about leaving there, quitting if necessary.

He said to me, "If I leave there then there wouldn't be any Christians in my department." Meaning, in his custodial department [where] he works, it is a group of Muslims who practice Islam and have a prayer closet at the school, he told me. They would speak their language when in a group and Chet never knew what was being said. He asked me, "Who would show them what it's like to walk with Jesus?" He said to me, "I guess I better stay."

He never ceases to amaze me as does our Lord, our God. Even now with all his struggles, he was keeping God in front. How do I argue that with him?

2BeCourageous updated their status.
November 09, 2012 – 4:28 a.m.

Today, we see a specialist first thing this morning—a doctor that specializes in Cognitive Disorders. I'm not sure what to hope for. We need a concrete written diagnosis of early-onset Alzheimer's (EOA). There, I said it. Do I want this? No! I don't want that diagnosis at all. I have been sick to my stomach all night not knowing how to pray for this. God's will couldn't be for my husband to have EOA. He has something terribly wrong though. (We needed the diagnosis for him to qualify for Social Security Disability.) I'm so scared, thank God I have Jake living with me, he keeps me grounded and thinking clearly. He always looks for a positive in all this to help his mom's fear and lack of patience, and, I'm sure, to comfort himself and his own fears. He has taken the brunt of my frustrations lately and, oh, how I beg for your forgiveness, my dear son.

Please, if you read this, pray for wisdom of the doctor and clarity for us all. More testing and another specialist appointment in a few months.

NOTE: *This is the doctor I wrote about in Chapter One, and he thought then it was early-onset Alzheimer's, but does not specialize in that field and wanted another doctor to make the call.*

2BeCourageous updated their status.
November 17, 2012

It's been a long night; Chet has been sick with a sinus infection for several days, well, until we went to the primary care doctor yesterday for it and he was suddenly cured! What the heck! So, then, last night, he couldn't stop coughing and the doctor gave him nothing because he told her he was on the mend, and, of course, it's viral.

He got up at 4:00 a.m. and started shaving and getting ready for work. I asked, "What are you doing its only 4:00 a.m.?"

He said, "Getting ready for work, I have to be there at eight."

I said, "You have three and a half hours yet." He just kept on getting ready. I had to tell him the time several times to try and make him aware.

Then he yells loudly, "OH NOOO!"

Of course, I jump up to find out what is wrong. He LOST his wedding ring. He had, of course, no idea when or where. I tried to look at the bright side, "WE CAN GET NEW ONES!" (Mine was cut off me for a surgery). Little did he know I have a ring picked out. HA!

Well, he wandered for three hours, looking lost and just so out of it. I think he took too much cough medicine that I gave him. He insisted on going to work. He had missed three days already being sick.

He put his gloves on to go out the door and yelled, "HEY! HEY!" He pulled his hand out of the glove and [voila]! His wedding ring was back on his finger! (Laughing) It had slid off into his glove. Too funny but sad, now how will I get my new ring?! (Laughing) Shows he is losing weight, his ring is very loose now, so he put it on his right hand instead; it fits tighter on that hand. I had never seen Chet like this before like he was this morning. I'm really nervous about him driving today. Ugh!

2BeCourageous updated their status.
November 25, 2012 – 6:31 a.m.

My husband was at his worst yesterday late afternoon and evening. When he is physically tired and mentally overtired, I notice he becomes worse. Jake and I have tried to talk him into applying for disability, but he will not agree to it! He feels he is fine; he said his only problem is he cannot remember names of people he knows. I do not know what to do. I will seek advice on Monday. His primary care physician (PCP) is getting him Aricept samples. This will be his first treatment for this mind-stealing disease.

I feel so helpless over this disease that has entered our house. My son, I fear, feels trapped into a situation he is trying his darnedest to make positive in any way he can. For an eighteen-year-old, that is darn amazing. I have days I want to tell him "run, get out now" to set him free from this responsibility he has taken on. I am blessed he is here, but worry about him. (End of this blog post.)

Jake described Alzheimer's best to me when he said, "The brain has many rooms like a house. Each room has its lights on, and, one by one, Alzheimer's walks through the house and turns off one light at a time, and, when all the lights are off in that room, the door slams shut and what was inside is forgotten. Room after room, the lights go out until the whole house is dark and you no longer can see inside." I thought that was a good way to describe it. Smart guy!

For Chet, early-onset Alzheimer's attacked his speech, his memories, his body functions; urinary tract infections were common. The sinuses drained for some reason when he ate. His hearing got very sensitive, and he startled and was jumpy very easily, and he got cold. Everything the brain controls seems to short circuit. It eats at each piece of you little by little, or very quickly as in my husband's case. Its symptoms are neither curable nor can you slow the progression of it.

The caregivers must live in the Alzheimer's World for that is the only way to get along with the person with dementia. Their reality is no longer your reality, and, if you don't enter their world to make it calmer for them, well, it becomes a lot harder. This is where "Do not argue with the person with dementia" comes in. They believe what they believe, and you can't change that; it will only heighten the tension and arguing. This is easier said than done! Don't argue was, by far, the hardest thing for me to follow;

I think I felt I could argue sense back into him. My children lived this with me and were not the only teens living with a parent or grandparent with dementia in the home.

Today's teens are tomorrow's caregivers as the American Baby Boomers are coming of age. Alzheimer's is the most common types of dementia, along with Lewy body dementia, vascular dementia, frontotemporal dementia, and others. Dementia is a group of symptoms of diseases like Alzheimer's and frontotemporal, Lewy body, etc., not a disease in itself. Education and awareness for the youth of today is vital. The dementia diseases are happening younger and younger.

Depending on where you go on the Internet, you will see there are different stages of Alzheimer's and other dementia diseases. I've noticed our doctors used three stages of mild, moderate, and late with the symptoms broken down for each stage. I can only tell you about Chet's symptoms because everyone is different.

I have to wonder, is Alzheimer's increasing in numbers as much as they say? Or is it people are being diagnosed less with mental health type diseases that was Alzheimer's all along? In the past, mental institutions were packed with people with dementia-type symptoms of all ages. Just something to think about.

"I have said these things to you, that in me you may have peace. In the world, you will have tribulation. But take heart; I have overcome the world."

JOHN 16:33 ESV

CHAPTER 6

BLESSINGS AMONGST THE CHAOS

2BeCourageous updated their status.
November 28, 2012 – 11:19 p.m.

It has been a very hard week. I'm so tired from it! Chet was supposed to go on Aricept, but the doctor or nurse has not gotten back to us yet. They were going to go through several boxes of medication samples that came in to see if it was in any of the boxes. You know it's expensive when the company has on their website a financial aid program for the drug. We'll be filling that out for sure!

2BeCourageous updated their status.
December 10, 2012 – 11:46 p.m.

Last week, I notified two of Chet's bosses that he has early-onset Alzheimer's. I told them that he has been having struggles at work for some time, and, even though he did not want me to tell them, I felt the need.

I could not take him coming home late at night distraught over this job anymore. They put him on a second shift by himself. It became very apparent over the weekend as we moved into an apartment, and the amount of stress on this immediate household, that he had gotten worse. I am not proud at all to say my patience have been slim to none. Some days I do not know where to find strength between my physical pain from my back and fibromyalgia. The mental pain that comes with all this and watching Chet's struggle, and how it pains him to accept what is happening to him. I assume it does; he won't talk about it at all. I went behind his back and wrote a letter to his bosses. I felt it was for his best interest.

Today, I got a call from one of his bosses saying he got the letter I sent and he so wished he would have known this all sooner. He explained how he has seen Chet change and how his work is not like it used to be. To make a long call short, he was very understanding and compassionate. He said Chet could go on unemployment (I took that to mean they would let him go, so he could qualify) and apply for disability, he said. Or, they could put him back on days (which I requested in the letter), strictly in the lunch room. He would be doing cleanup and being with the students (which Chet likes), but only those hours. So, this would cut his hours down to maybe three to four a day. I told his boss that he could not collect unemployment and qualify for disability. It's not allowed they would deny him quickly. He agreed he could go to cafeteria if Chet agreed and asked me to talk to him first, then call him so he can talk to him tomorrow.

When I told Chet, he got defensive until I said his boss had nothing but his best interest at heart with the phone call. Long story short, my husband agreed to the cafeteria with delight and relief! He hated working nights in the dark, empty halls of the school.

Something Chet did from the start was he would bring home food from the cafeteria that was left over—I'm assuming—off kid's plates that were not touched, mostly hash browns and apples. He would bring them home by the bags full. He never could stand to see food go to waste. The apples we made into apple sauce. Much of the other stuff we discarded when he wasn't around.

I remember being in the mall with Chet and we were walking hand in hand; the area was known to be rough. These three big, strapping guys are walking towards us, and they look tough. I'm getting nervous and, suddenly, they smile and one says, "Mr. Chet, it's so good to see you, how ya doing?" They shook his hand and gave him man hugs. They were students from the school, and they just loved him. He was that way, a lovable guy, everyone liked him. It did my heart so good to witness this.

After much number punching to show Chet the Social Security benefits he could get, we are going to file for disability with his approval. Doing so does not mean he has accepted this disease at all. But after much stormy weather within the house this weekend, I reassured him, I'm a storm chaser, not a runner, and I would not be going anywhere ever but by his side. I promised him I would keep him home no matter what and that the whole family is rooting for him and love him.

At first, after the call from his boss, I felt I sabotaged our financial welfare and his well-being. I mean, we are right at Christmas, fifteen days out; I have no money for food, let alone to buy my husband a gift or my children or my grandson. I have nothing to make it meaningful or outstanding, so that he can have a memory to last. What will his last memory be?

I know Christmas is about Jesus Christ, our Savior. I know we celebrate Him every year with a cake. We have always made a big to-do over Christmas, one of my favorite holidays. I guess this could end up being our Christmas miracle. For I did not know how to pull off our survival of waiting for disability for him. I think him working part-time is God answering prayer. God is good!

During this time, we moved into a small apartment to save money because we will have a five- or six-month waiting period for SSD to kick in. Chessie and Brandon and the baby had moved in with his parents during the first quarter of 2012 when tensions got high with the kids, and adjusting to Chet's new problems with his dementia was hard on all of us. Plus, we had a major ant problem, and Chessie discovered some in her bed one night and that was it. She fell apart. All the built-up emotion came pouring out in tears. It was for the best that they went to his parents' house. I could no longer support them financially. I felt horrible about it all, but it turned out for the best for all of us. So, it was now Jake, Chet, and myself.

2BeCourageous updated their status.
December 28, 2012 – 6:02 a.m.

Well, we are now almost to the New Year. Chet left his job at the school and I panicked even more inside, but this was so healthy for him. He hated it and was having trouble with it. But, to apply for Social Security Disability, he cannot have a job, I learned. The church job also let him go, so he could qualify for his disability and they, too, noticed the changes in him. So, I got on my knees and prayed.

Well, guess what? We made it through Christmas and God blessed us! Blessed us with each other! Chet, Jake, Chessie, Brandon, and Braydon were all here with me on Christmas Eve. Our traditional day to celebrate. My mother in Michigan had sent us a honey baked ham for Christmas, and I saved it especially for Christmas Eve. What a wonderful gift that was. She knows my heart—FOOD! We did have to make the humbling trip to the food bank. My heart was heavy over this but they blessed us so. I had enough from there to make a whole meal, a feast for our Christmas Eve. Even a pie! God does take care of His people. Then, the day after the trip to the food bank, we received an unexpected gift that brought tears to my eyes.

We had no idea how we would pay our life insurance and a couple of other late bills, but the life insurance had us sick. I was going on two months behind. The gift made it possible to pay it up, so it went back in effect and paid on another bill. Plus, I could buy a small gift for each person. On top of that, someone gave me several used toys for Braydon's age that was good as new, and I could clean them up and wrap them up for him. God so answered prayer. God is good! I cannot change what health situation we have here, but God will bring us through it! We also received a chocolate cake and Chessie made sure before they left that we were all going to sing "Happy Birthday" to Jesus, which has been a tradition since they were born with cake and candles. She is starting Braydon in the same tradition and that so made my heart sing!

May you all see the true meaning of this season and hold tight to your family and may you all have a Happy New Year! God bless. (End post.)

Chet had been driving back and forth to work, and I would pray every time he got behind the wheel. When driving with him, he would get confused, and, if you told him suddenly he missed the exit, he would slam on the brakes on the highway and not know what to do. He even went up a wrong way on a ramp. It was time to stop driving, but I wasn't sure how to approach it with him. I had heard so many stories of people with dementia not wanting to give up the keys and having arguments over it. I just decided I would always offer to drive, and I got very lucky because he was fine with that and never asked to drive again. I think he knew he was a danger on the road but we didn't have to discuss it, and he was fine about me driving everywhere. That was one big battle that never happened.

The beginning of 2013 brought much paperwork and new testing set up by Social Security Disability (SSD). He had to see a medical doctor assigned by SSD and a psychologist for mental testing. The psychologist exam, I wasn't allowed to be with Chet, but I could hear them in the other room. He wasn't doing well and the doctor cut it short. She came out to me and asked me what he was diagnosed with because he didn't understand any of the questions. I told her early-onset Alzheimer's. She said, "Well, that makes sense then because he doesn't understand what I want from him." For once, this was a good thing because her recommendation was he get SSD! The medical doctor also could tell right away that Chet was not well and he, too, must have put in Chet's favor because Chet was approved in February within four weeks of applying.

If it is your first time applying for Social Security Disability for your loved one, get all their medical records from every doctor they have seen in the last two years and send those to SSD with your application. Early-onset Alzheimer's is on the Social Security Disability Compassionate list, which speeds the process from eighteen months to four to eight weeks for a decision, depending on how fast your doctors fill out the forms sent to them.

I had Chet's sisters write letters to SSD, detailing how they saw Chet change and go downhill. They sent them to me and I put that in the package with the application and medical records. My children and I also wrote letters to talk about the decline in Chet and what we have seen wrong with him. They went in with the application. On the application, don't hold back on the bad things your loved one does; tell it like it is. Doing the extra mile with records and letters and filling out the application with everything he can't do anymore got him approved in four weeks.

You must stay on top of the doctors, though, and don't be afraid to ask each doctor for a letter also, that they see your loved one as disabled and why. The extra letter, plus their report, only helps. I did the same routine when I applied for my disability—sent letters and sent copies of my charts from doctors. It's a stressful time going through it, but it must be done.

Since we are talking about filing paperwork, I can't encourage you enough to complete your wills, power of attorney for financial, and power of attorney for health, and living will. Do these things as soon as you can; do not wait. Your loved will only get worse and may be unable to understand or sign for them if you wait too long. I got all my legal forms off Dave Ramsey's website. They have forms for every state, and it's 100% legal and much cheaper than hiring a lawyer. You need a notary and, if you have a friend who is a notary, ask them to help you get the papers signed. The signatures must be done in front of a notary. Banks have notaries.

"O my Strength, I will sing praises to you, for you, O God, are my fortress, the God who shows me, steadfast love."

PSALM 59:17 ESV

CHAPTER 7

PRAISING YOU IN THIS STORM

There were days when you question God, how could this happen to the most wonderful man there was? My personal belief on this is God doesn't make illness happen. He is as heartbroken as we are; illness is part of the world we live in. He does miracles, we have had a few now in our lives. But even though I prayed for a cure and didn't receive it, I do get sad but I don't get mad at God. I can only attribute that to my husband teaching me to have faith and trust in God. I'd never seen him mad at God, not once. I always believed that God would make Chet whole again once he was in Heaven. That's the miracle. Even with the illness, Chet had never blamed God or gotten mad at Him.

A huge help to me that had gotten me through many nights were friends I made in dementia support groups on Facebook. They are for caregivers, family, and the people with dementia. I have met some amazing people in these Facebook groups and learned so much from them. You don't feel so alone when you can go online and talk to others dealing with the same things. It's all private and no one from the outside of the group members can see your posts. Many of my prayer warriors come from these groups, and you also become friends on your own pages with many people from these groups. A lot of great advice also from these people because they have been there. The four I belong to are "Forget Me Not," "Dementia Aware" (out of the UK), "Early Onset Alzheimer's Support Group," and "Frontotemporal Dementia Info and Support." I will put links in the back of the book so you can join them if you wish.

2BeCourageous updated their status.
February 26, 2013 – 4:38 p.m.
PRAISE … I'm jumping the gun, I have not gotten an official letter but I called Social Security Disability and Chet was APPROVED yesterday—but it went back for a review (they pull random ones to be reviewed before the letter goes out, lucky us).

So, he is approved and he will get Social Security Income (different than disability) to help us live for six months until he gets his first Social Security Disability check in, maybe, June which is paid in July. Ready for the amount to help us live? $28.00 a month—we are living now! Okay, they add that to my check amount and that reaches the max you can have for Social Security Income (SSI). His Social Security Disability checks will support us once June check comes. Thank you, Lord. We have survived since December with no income from him and no unemployment. I know God will see us through until June! God gifted us from an outside source that is lending a hand during these months of waiting. Praise God. Thank you to those who have been praying for us!

2BeCourageous updated their status.
February 28, 2013 – 11:31 p.m.
I have noticed that with disease comes estrangement of friendships and even family. I have noticed not just within our tribulations, but many others go through this also. You find out who your friends are for sure.

2BeCourageous updated their status.
March 25, 2013 – 7:22 a.m.

Well, I didn't post on here about my recent trip I went on, though most of you know from my Heidi DeBoer page.

What a trip and vacation I got to have. I rolled my ankle in a shallow hole or dip in the grass at the apartment. It was enough to turn the ankle with a shattering snap and bone trying to poke through the skin. I remember cute ambulance drivers that were very sweet. They gave me an injection for pain in the ambulance. I broke three bones. In ER, they put me to sleep to set the bones, and I woke up what seemed like seconds ... all wrapped and snug as a bug.

My fall was at 8:00 in the morning on Wednesday, the 20th of March 2013. That evening, still in ER, I had a three-hour surgery to put plates and pins and whatnots in. I was told I stopped breathing and they had to put me on something to help me breathe, and, boy, I can tell they put something down my throat. I have not had TMJ troubles for years and my jaw was killing me.

It is now Monday, the 25th; I'm still at Stonecrest Medical Center in Smyrna, TN. My blood pressure dropped too low last night after jumping high. I'm thinking it's all the medications interacting with each other. I'm supposed to stay for a couple of weeks at a rehab center in Smyrna, TN. The pain is throbbing today, and having chronic back pain doesn't help to be on your back most of the day. I need to learn to get around with no weight bearing on the left foot. I must hop with a walker. I felt going to rehab to learn to hop seemed stupid. Until I couldn't take myself up a small step into the shower at the hospital. It's just my brain couldn't process how to make it happen.

Chet has been my loyal mate by my side, sleeping here on a cot. I sense the need from him to be my hero and protect me, or perhaps that is what I need from him. He insisted he stay again last night so he could hear firsthand what the doctor says and where I'm being transported. (The hospital did not want to send me home right away because of Chet's dementia. They didn't want me to deal with that until I could get around on my own.) He will not remember what the doctor says tomorrow. But today his need is to be part and involved in this process. It's an unspoken need but, being in tune with him, I know it's there. Words cannot express how much I love this man and how much I already miss pieces of him.

Chet has always been my hero, saving the day like the time I lost my diamond on my ring while on a trip to Virginia. We took a family trip to Virginia to see Grandma Nazha, my dear friend who became our adopted grandma to the kids. She lived in the Shenandoah Valley. Just gorgeous with the mountains all around.

Chet and I and the kids decided to go to the Caverns in Front Royal not far away and drive up on Skyline Drive in the mountains. We did the caverns first. I love going into the caves and tour them with guides. There was a slope that was gravel, and I had Chessie's—age six—hand and old grace here slipped and fell and took Chessie down with me. We were okay, just embarrassed! There were some amazing sites in those caves and we enjoyed them. We also walked the grounds and looked at what was there.

Next, Skyline Drive. We got up there and stopped at every overlook to see the sites. We were having a great time; it was so pretty looking down in the valley. I was sitting in the car and I glanced down and noticed my engagement ring—the diamond was gone! My heart sank and I started screaming and, eventually, crying. We stopped at every overlook we had visited and searched the grounds—nothing! We went back to the caverns and searched the grounds there. At that point, I was begging God to help me find it; help me find this material thing that meant so much to me. It was gravel and stones everywhere. How would we find it? I prayed some more. Then Chet got the idea that I had fallen in the cave and maybe it was in there. I said to him, "We were way deep into the caves when I fell. How would we find the exact spot? It was dark and would they let us back in to look?"

Well, two guides let Chet go and look. They went with him with flashlights to the spot he was sure where I fell at. They searched the grounds and gravel stones. I sat in the car pouting and crying when all three finally came out and up to the car. The female guide said, "We are sorry, but we could not find it, but we will keep an eye out for it on our tours. We're sorry." As I teared up more, Chet stepped forward and opened his hand and there was my diamond! They found it! They tricked me! Mean! HA! They went to the spot where Chet thought I fell and, as they were looking and flashing their flashlights, a reflection came off a little ledge where a handrail was bolted on to. There, on that little ledge, sat my diamond. God made that happen; I'm totally convinced with no doubts. Chet was my hero! God too!

2BeCourageous updated their status.
March 26, 2013 – 11:07 p.m.
At rehab, which is really a nursing home. I'm so sad, my roommate who was eighty-two (probably the average age here at the nursing home) has cards and photos all over her side of the room and pretty frilly things. Do you know what the only thing on the wall on my side was? A calendar from a funeral home! (Laughing) I kid you not! Who does that in a nursing home? I took a photo and will post it when I ever have Wi-Fi again. One computer in the whole place with the Internet and it's OLD and SLOW. I sure wish my side of the room had cards and things and whatnots to hang on the board and wall, besides a funeral home ad. (Laughing)

2BeCourageous updated their status.
March 28, 2013 – 5:43 p.m.
Whoop, whoop! GOING HOME, 8:00 a.m. on Friday! Wonderful, Medicaid will not pay the co-pays my health insurance will start charging this weekend for rehab. I never thought I'd be happy about insurance not paying something. I WANT OUT OF HERE! So, I must do outpatient PT and OT three times a week. My husband has been taking wonderful care of me and getting things done, he and Jake together!

2BeCourageous updated their status.

April 10, 2013 – 2:45 p.m.

Our trials and journeys continue living in a world of dementia, but life must proceed forward also. We, as in Jake and I, are in the process of filling out an application for Motion Picture/Television Production at the Academy of Art University San Francisco, four-year program. Jake is a natural at directing films. He and his sister have been making movies since they were around eight years old. Jake has decided to do online courses for now, so he can be here with his dad. I think there is an inner fear, maybe Chet will forget him if he goes to San Francisco, but perhaps not. Jake won a $2000.00 scholarship for his film portfolio he sent into the school. Very proud of this guy.

2BeCourageous updated their status.

April 10, 2013 – 3:06 p.m.

I haven't posted a lot on here, not a lot good. I've been so sick again four to five hours at a time at night with constant sweating until I'm soaked, and restless leg syndrome has turned into major locked up spasms in my legs. A severe constant need to move them. I see a doctor, my sleep neurologist on Friday.

It's hard to be patient with each other when I'm whining and sick, and Chet is not understanding my needs and gets extra confused. He wants to help me—God bless his heart! Then we fight over little things such as control of the wheelchair … ahhh (laughing). I don't want to go in this direction, stupid stuff we shouldn't even be getting sensitive about. My problem, I'm too independent. They tell me don't climb the stairs—look, I'm at the top! HA! Don't go out the door, the wheelchair will get stuck. Ha! Look at me; I'm out on the sidewalk alone in the wheelchair! I'm such a brat!

Chet is so bored, so I'm going to let him push me on the concrete trails at the park today. I can't use crutches, per doctor's orders, so I haven't. With the walker, I die twenty steps out hopping. In the parking lot, my brain says jump up the curb with the walker, but my body stands and stares at the curb saying, "Are you nuts?" The doctor won't give me a kneel-on type board device to get around on. Something to do with the pressure pressing on the leg. I do well getting around. My husband is wonderful; it's me! I'm whining, but thank God for Facebook where I can whine if I want too.

Heidi DeBoer updated her status.
April 24, 2013 – 5:37 p.m.
Well, my body had a pain party today. I would have sent invitations, but it was a surprise party. I woke up—SURPRISE! I couldn't move. The ankle's been great today, except I took a nap and took the Frankinboot off to let some air on the leg. I fell asleep and woke up screaming, scared Chet and I both. My foot must have had an involuntary jerk back; man, the pain in the ankle shot up my spine.

NOTE TO SELF AND OTHERS: KEEP BOOT ON IN BED LIKE TOLD TO DO. (Laughing)

2BeCourageous updated their status.
May 10, 2013 – 6:45 p.m.
I'm having a very hard time at night still, the four hours or more of restless-leg-turned-restless-body syndrome. Found out it is called a name ending with the word disease. Yay! I needed another disease. (Laughing) Besides being tortured with this nightly ordeal of thrashing and uncontrollable limb movement and joint and muscle pain, I'm groaning and chanting like I'm possessed to help keep my sanity intact during the attacks; it must be a coping thing. I'm sure I'm driving my boys insane with it. Pray for all of us to get through another night

Next week, if I live through four more nights, I see a new specialist on Tuesday for neuromuscular neuropathy. Chet has been a trooper. I get such pain and exhaustion, and, with each attack, he will massage my muscles for hours. I have noticed a loving willingness to try and help me through these from my husband. Almost like it makes him feel needed. Does he know how needed he is? Does he know that his being is my being? Does he know I adore him? I tell him often! He needs to feel useful and needed. We all do, but when you are losing your memory and abilities, your need becomes even greater to feel helpful. Man, I need to find a different way than having these insane attacks at night to help him feel helpful. Ugh.

Heidi DeBoer updated her status.
May 20, 2013 – 9:44 p.m.

Well, today was two months from the great ankle break. Went to see the surgeon today and took more x-rays. He said the ankle looks great, and he said he saw me walk in with my mega boot on and no walker. He said I'm doing good and progressing fast.

So, I was ready for him to say no more boot and into the ankle lace up brace.

I must wear the boot anytime I leave the house until three and a half months from surgery, so another month and a half. I have to wear the lace up in the house. He gave me a cane and I need to use it in and out of the house. Boooo.

He said, "Slow down, you aren't healed, you had surgery on both sides of your ankle and you can re-break it very easily." What? It's not a bionic ankle? But I'm a movin' kind of girl! (Laughing)

2BeCourageous updated their status.
May 24, 2013 – 1:16 p.m.

Chet had on the movie *The Notebook* when I came downstairs at the beginning. Yes, now I'm crying; it has a whole new meaning after watching it this time around. Is this our future? If so, I want the end of our story to end like Alley's and Noah's ... (spoiler alert), knowing each other, holding each other, side by side, waking up in Heaven together.

2BeCourageous updated their status.
May 24, 2013 – 6:58 p.m.

I don't know what to think, Chet is so different the last few weeks or so. In a good way. He brings up past things with no problem. Meaning, years past. I'm thinking, *You remember that? I hardly remember that.* He remembers what he has done in the past week. I haven't had to repeat a story or event all week; he even smiles more. He looks at me with calmness, with no tension in his face, and he smiles at me in a loving way that I have longed for so long. It tells me I have his heart. He jokes and laughs with us; he even gets Jake's and my silliness. (Laughing) That's not always easy. We hold hands while we sit on the couch and there is a warmth as he reached for my hand to hold while we walk in public again. (Yes, I'm walking with a cane now.) He isn't jumping in a fearful way when I reach for him (a trait of Alzheimer's), he is accepting and calm.

I'm seeing my husband that I have missed so much. I'm afraid, for this illness is very cruel. It gives and takes away so quickly; it leaves you wanting these moments to last forever. Then it rears its ugliness, and it's gone. The security of his smile is saying, "I love you no matter what." The sparkle in his eye that tells me I'm safe and we can beat whatever tries to take us down. His look and a smile can say so much with no words needed. Please, dementia, you vicious trick player, leave my man alone, he is mine! You may claim his mind but I will always claim his heart.

2BeCourageous updated their status.
May 26, 2013 – 4:36 p.m.

Well, I saw my sleep neurologist over a week ago, she was in hopes that the horrible restless body attacks were withdrawal from coming off the medication I am on for restless legs. I am on it for restless legs, but it makes me tired, I fall asleep everywhere. My head dropped in my cereal bowl one morning, fell asleep. So much for the weaning off from it process. Just knock me out the next time I quit a drug that needs to be weaned off from. Well, each night gets better and better.

I feel like a new person being off that drug. I lessened some other medications, and the neurologist whom I like very much restarted one med I stopped months ago, thinking it was to blame for my illness. Then, my mom sent me some restless leg cream with magnesium and vitamin

E and lavender and a ton of other stuff in it. No restless body attacks for almost two weeks and no mild restless legs for three nights and I'm sleeping all night since off that drug. Life is lovely.

Heidi DeBoer updated her status.
June 11, 2013 – 12:19 p.m.
I saw my psychiatrist MD for the first time since I was hospitalized with the broken ankle. Have to see him every two months for medications. I have made major changes in my meds on my own that has made major improvements in my life by quitting some and lowering others. Chet laughed when we left. He said, "You just walked in there told him what you did and said give me this and that dose. He wrote it, and you left!"

Heidi DeBoer updated her status.
June 11, 2013 – 7:43 p.m.
I think this is my 8th week in physical therapy they increased the bike to level 3, and I beat my best time at 1.8 miles in 8 min. They don't make me go fast it's just me challenging myself each time. Been pushing myself on all the exercises and I feel wonderful and losing weight. I feel a Madagascar Move It, Move It, dance coming on. Chet comes with me to every appointment, gets him out of the house.

2BeCourageous updated their status.
July 05, 2013 – 12:52 p.m.
I have learned I should not argue with Chet, but I have not yet hit my head against the wall enough for I still slip up. He does not yet ask things over and over hourly, but, when he doesn't understand, I fall back into the trap of thinking he should understand (no, he shouldn't). I have my life-long problem of not only repeating the exact same way I said it before that he didn't understand the first time, but saying it three times louder like he went suddenly deaf. I must learn to live in the Alzheimer's World, and I must learn not to get frustrated. He cannot help what he gets and doesn't get; he has a brain disease. It's up to me to make his world pleasant.

"So, all of us who have had that veil removed can see and reflect the glory of the Lord. And the Lord—who is the Spirit—makes us more and more like him as we are changed into his glorious image."

2 CORINTHIANS 3:18 NLT

CHAPTER 8

REFLECTIONS FROM THE MIRROR WITHIN

I was sitting on my front steps earlier today, cooling down and trying to get the bleach out of my lungs after washing down the bathroom. It was beautiful outside, looking at the leaves on the trees. Seeing our neighbor's pasture a few houses down with the horses in it brought me back when we raised horses and owned a small horse farm. Good memories.

I was also brought back to the days before I met Chet and I worked at TMC Ranch, a racehorse breeding ranch. Guys oversaw breeding and worked the ranch (the dirty work); the girls groomed, did medical, and trained the horses. You had to earn your way up the ladder to ride and train the horses. I loved horses and I feared them. After all, they are a 1000+ pound animal that kick, bite, run you over, and are high off the ground. An adrenaline rush for sure. I had just got promoted to being allowed to ride. Yeah, riding the oldest, most stubborn gray gelding to pony on (meaning ride on with a young horse at your side on a lead rope to exercise them). But yes! I get to ride finally!

I did not get along with this horse; he had attitude, he was set in his ways and didn't listen or respond to me very well. I did not like him! I got mad one day and said to my boss, who was the head trainer, "This horse is stupid, I've never been on such a dumb animal, and he is so slow!" (I was mad since the day I was assigned him to ride and pony with him because he wasn't one of the cool horses others were on.)

She looked up at me on him and said, "A horse is like a mirror." She walked away.

I asked, "What the heck does that mean?"

She said, "The horse is a reflection of the rider on its back."

I sat there, not happy with her response but pondered it for a while. Later, to my surprise, she made me and another girl who worked there go out in the indoor arena, get on our horses bareback, and the three of us had to play tag at a run with a rolled up newspaper in one hand to tag with. We could not let the other one touch us.

I thought to myself, *This horse will never do this and that I'm going to die!* They suddenly took off! My horse took off at a run when I asked him. But I pulled back to slow him and Lee, my boss, smacked me in the head with her newspaper. My mouth opened and all I could do was laugh! Now, I was determined. I leaned forward, clicked my mouth, and just slightly tapped his rib and he charged straight for them as asked and turned sharp and spun out-of-the-way when asked. This was so not the same horse—what happened? I was still on and surprised by that when I connected my newspaper on my friend and took off in a new direction. I was running bareback and what's amazing to me was that I was still on! My horse stayed under me! He was so smooth, this horse was so into this, and I was having a blast suddenly. He and I were working with each other as a team, not against each other. I was the one in training that day. I enjoyed riding him after that. I had gained confidence and respect for the old guy.

Did the horse change? No—I did. It was my attitude he was picking up on; it was my lack of confidence he could feel. My fear, I wasn't trying, I wasn't doing what I'd been taught. He was responding to me; he reflected my fears, attitude, and behavior.

Sitting on the steps, I thought how being a Christian is so much like that. We are the mirrors; we are to reflect Jesus' love and forgiveness. As Christians, others are looking at us and into us, watching us, and doing what we do. If we don't have the right attitude, the confidence, the love, we don't reflect well onto others. We need to reflect Jesus in our daily lives.

Many times, my husband with his dementia had negative responses, reactions, and emotions that were fueled by my attitude. He had frustration because of the way I chose to react to things he said or did that he could no way help. When I took the horse by the reigns, meaning choosing better ways to respond to him and not let my fear and bad attitude win, we became a team.

When I reflect Jesus in my home life, things are smoother, but, some days, we just must stop and pray for a better tomorrow.

"Anxiety in a man's heart weighs him down, but a good word makes him glad."

PROVERBS 12:25 ESV

CHAPTER 9

GOOD SPELL, BAD SPELL

2BeCourageous updated their status.
July 14, 2013 – 12:46 a.m.

In the eyes of our nineteen-month-old grandson, Braydon, my husband is perfect in mind and body. Braydon will run up to him and give him hugs and kisses, and the hugs and kisses he gets back from grandpa say it all. They are each other's world at those moments.

2BeCourageous updated their status.
July 16, 2013 – 1:54 a.m.

We spent the day at Opry Mills in Nashville [for] well over five hours with our twins, Jake and Chessie, and our grandson, nineteen-month-old old Braydon. By hour four, I'm pooped out; I'm still using the cane and the kids want to hit several more stores. Then Chet tells me he is having a good time, which made me so happy that I continued on to more stores. He gets so bored doing nothing all day, no yard to putter in; we just haven't even had gas money for so long. We couldn't go anywhere. Now that his checks have started (SSD), we can get out more.

I found myself on the nervous side today at the mall; it was never "Where is Braydon?" but "Where is Dad?" He'd be behind me and I'd ask, "Where's Dad?" But if I wasn't, I noticed Jake saying it too. It's just we have no cell phones, we had to give them up until we can afford them again. I worry he will get confused or lost and I can't call him. I need to relax but, see, there will come a day he will get confused and lost, it wasn't today, and life was good. God is good all the time.

Heidi DeBoer shared her photo.
July 20, 2013 – 12:55 p.m.
Twenty-two years ago today, at 1:30 p.m., I married my cowboy in a Western style wedding, and though happily ever after is only in fairy tales, I've never regretted this man once. I love him more than my words can say. God knew we were right for each other and made it happen. His faith and trust in God brought so much to my life. Love you, Chet DeBoer. Happy anniversary!

2BeCourageous updated their status.
July 22, 2013 – 5:47 a.m.
My husband has been in a very good spell for well over a month if not more. That has changed big time this past week. Goodbye good spell, hello bad spell. I will check his blood sugar when he gets up. Yesterday, he couldn't find me a good six plus times in Kroger. I'd tell him I'm going down this aisle, he'd blink and he couldn't figure out where I was. He doesn't understand given directions; you must ask him three different ways for him to get it. I don't know if it's the big space of the store that he doesn't recognize me at a distance or what the problem was. Sometimes we were in the same aisle, yet he was calling for me, lost. We both became frustrated with each other today. I get my hopes up when he does well. I then think, maybe they (the doctors) are wrong. Or I think, if this is as bad as it gets, this is so doable. I need to get on him about medication. He

tells me he took it when in fact he didn't. He isn't lying, he really believes he took it. Another lesson learned on trusting what he says.

2BeCourageous updated their status.
August 11, 2013 – 11:59 p.m.

Another week has started, which means another week has ended; nothing remarkable really happened last week. He was very frustrated with me today at the grocery store. (Due to car expense and college expense getting my son registered for his second semester of college and his editing program cost, Jake is paying me back in September or October when his funds get sent, so the money is short now.) Chet was picking things out and putting them in the cart. A lot of things! I don't have enough money to buy food for the whole month. He does not know this. I could tell him this but it brings on a worry he does not need. If he is worried or scared, his symptoms seem to exasperate.

I did explain the budget is tight and I cannot buy what he was picking out. This is where I made my mistake. He pouted and was annoyed then. If I were up on my game, I would have let him at least have one of his items. Then ask him also to help me pick out the items I needed, letting him choose which ones. I screwed up. I wasn't living in the Alzheimer's World at that moment, I was in my world of worry and trying to get it done fast. I don't like seeing him feel hurt. I need to make better decisions how I handle things next time.

****

Jake commented on this status and said to me, "The five of us will get through this together, Mom."

I asked him, "Five? Who is the fifth?"

He said, "God, Mom. He is helping us get through this." Just like his dad, directing me back to God.

"But in your hearts revere Christ as Lord. Always be prepared to give an answer to everyone who asks you to give the reason for the hope that you have. But do this with gentleness and respect, keeping a clear conscience, so that those who speak maliciously against your good behavior in Christ may be ashamed of their slander."

1 Peter 3:15–16 NIV

I always thought, one day, my son would become a preacher! Yeah, I did! Because, at such a young age, he seemed to put on God's armor and march to the beat of his own drum out to save the world.

When Jake was little, he was, well, a lot like he is now—with a sense of humor, an entertainer, and he was not afraid to express his opinion and tell people what he thinks. Also, if he felt the need to share God, he would! He may be a little less aggressive about it now than when he was younger. In high school, he stood up for creation in one of his classes at school! He was told he is entitled to his opinion. He would make comments of proof about creation even when it wasn't very welcome. This, I think, delighted him. After watching a seven-DVD lecture on creation, he felt ready to take on evolution and the teachers who believed in it. Done so with respect.

I was thinking the other day what made him put on his armor so young and share his view of God? He talked about God to friends when he was in grade school. I was in awe of my son at a young age but worried at the same time of the bullying he could bring on himself from non--Christians. Even Christians can be mean.

I wondered what encouraged him because we were not ones to make them read their Bibles daily. We did go to church and we put them in Sunday school and youth groups. Chet would talk about God with them. We did family devotions but not daily when they were young. I was always amazed when Jake would come home and tell me how he talked about God in school today to so and so. Or he'd tell me, so and so was not a Christian.

I'd ask "How do you know?"

He'd say, "I asked them!" He had a better relationship with God at age seven than I did at that time, and it came so naturally for him. He had his struggles, though, many battles of low self-esteem, an ADD diagnosis, migraines, and a tender heart. But, in my eyes, he marched onward with his sword drawn.

My fondest, most humbling memory of my son was, I believe, when he was in fourth or fifth grade and was out in the park where we lived with friends. He came home in tears. I asked him what was wrong and he said the kids were passing cigarettes and he refused them. He told them that they needed to go to church and find God and not smoke anymore, that Jesus doesn't like that. They then made fun of him and called him names. Called him crazy and mean things.

Off the top of my head, without thinking it out, I said to him, "Jake do not talk to them anymore about God, they will make fun of you, just stay away from them." (Yeah, I know, brilliant—not!)

Well, he looked me right in the eye and said with tears, "Mom! If we don't save them who will?" Wow! I felt small at that moment, and my heart was in my throat! Now, I had tears too! I told him he was so right on! That maybe we could figure it out together, not alone! My heart was so proud of him! The cigarette issue took a back seat that day; he knew it was wrong and he knew not to try it. The kids, I didn't know if they were Christians; we saved no souls that day. I'm sure my son left a lasting impression that, maybe, someday they'll look back on. He left one on me forever.

"Train up a child in the way he should go: and when he is old, he will not depart from it."

PROVERBS 22:6 KJV

2BeCourageous updated their status.
August 16, 2013 – 10:08 p.m.

A rough few days, Chet's speech has declined, could be stress. We have argued a few times. No, I have fallen apart a few times, completely overwhelmed. I got frustrated over him not remembering significant people, and he reminded me, saying, "That is what is wrong with me. I have that thing that keeps me from remembering" (me—tears). That is the first time acknowledging his disease. When am I going to get this? Why do I let my fear take hold of me and react from it? Of course, it's fear. Will he not know me next? That is the ultimate cruelty of this disease. I hate you, Alzheimer's. I am my children's parent; I now find myself being the parent to my husband more than a wife. I don't like this. Sigh.

2BeCourageous updated their status.
August 31, 2013 – 10:59 a.m.

Every so often, I get the "Be nicer, you get mad too fast at Dad" lecture from my son who could be a diplomat. He has a talent of talking to people with suggestions for keeping the peace and working out solutions. I praise God for him even when I know I'm wrong and he is right, and it irritates me (laughing); don't tell him, it will go to his head.

Heidi DeBoer updated her status.
September 29, 2013 – 7:02 p.m.

Chet was happy when Jake and I got home from play practice at church. He was excited that he got to watch football all afternoon and that both his favorite teams won. The Detroit Lions, and the Titans, this made his day. #happyman

2BeCourageous updated their status.
October 10, 2013 – 3:48 p.m.

Offer accepted for a new home; we are buying a home in La Vergne on an acre. A place for Chet and us to call home and a big yard to putts around in. It's perfect for us.

Heidi DeBoer updated her status.

October 11, 2013 – 11:38 p.m.

Had a good day with hubby and baby boy, took the grandson to park and then McDonald's. He fell asleep in the car on the way home, and grandpa carried him inside, and the child slept almost four hours. Babysitting is so hard. Ha-ha.

Heidi DeBoer updated her status.

October 19, 2013 – 6:17 p.m.

We went to the American Indian Pow Wow today at Long Hunter Park with Chet and Jake and our friends, Darrell and Annie, and we got a bit cold but enjoyed the many craft booths and Indian Tacos and the dances and songs and costumes the American Indians compete and dance in. Chet and I try to go every year since we've been married. Chet really enjoys it.

2BeCourageous updated their status.

October 21, 2013 – 8:03 p.m.

I'm not big on sitting, watching sports on TV. We watched Michigan play Indiana last Saturday, guess what we are watching now? Michigan play Indiana from last Saturday.

    Me to Chet: "This is a repeat."

    Chet: "No it's not."

    Me: "The sun is shining."

    Chet: "No, it's dark out, what are you talking about?" and looks at me like I'm weird.

    Me: "I meant on TV, the sun is out at the game. It's night here."

    Chet: "Well, it's day there."

    Me: "It's in Michigan, it's night there too. I'm saying this is from Saturday, we have seen this." (Voice getting louder.)

    Chet: "I know."

    Me: "You know what?"

    Chet: "I've already seen this."

Me: "That's what I've been saying."

Chet: "Okay."

Me: "Let's change the channel."

Chet: "No, I want to see who wins." (Laughing)

Me: "Ahhhhhh!" (Laughing) You must learn to laugh, laugh at yourself, at them; find the funny things, make them laugh with you. We are a family of finding humor in the worst of life. You must, or you will go crazy or crazier.

2BeCourageous updated their status.
October 21, 2013 – 8:56 p.m.

If the walls of your house could speak, what stories would they tell?

Our walls would tell a love story but also some uncomplimentary stories of our lives and behaviors. The stories have not always been complimentary to Christ. Our early life story did not go per the way we planned our life together. Our current midlife story, though very unwelcome, I know we will stand with Christ and praise Him for our blessings and stand by each other no matter how the story goes. I learn more and more from my church and my support group network. With God in our corner, we can rewrite the story to make the best of what we have. To sit back, worry less, and enjoy the blessings we have. I hope I explained that right. Being a Christian doesn't mean perfection, that's why Christ came to wash away our sins through Him; we all mess up, it's through His grace we are saved.

Heidi DeBoer shared a status.
October 22, 2013 – 7:59 p.m.

Chessie has a new look—purple hair! Chet saw it and started singing "Purple Rain." Been married twenty-two years and I didn't even know he knew who Prince was, let alone the lyrics to his song. So, two surprises today—my daughter's purple hair and my husband singing a Prince song!

"A friend is always loyal, and a brother is born to help in time of need."

PROVERBS 17:17 NLT

CHAPTER 10

STIGMA

Lessons learned in the DeBoer house for some of us were finding out who our loyal friends and family were in the time of need. The loyal became the unexpected, and the expected became missing and too distant to want to be loyal and show support.

Webster's definition of stigma: "a set of negative and often unfair beliefs that a society or group of people have about something."

Diseases have a stigma; dementia, such as Alzheimer's, has a stigma. People do not know how to act or respond to the person with dementia. Some people fear it; it makes them uncomfortable to be around the person with dementia. Some people feel that the person with dementia won't remember them anyway if they come, so why bother. This is untrue! The person is aware. At least the first few years in our case. He hadn't seen or heard from certain people whom he was one-time close to; he was well aware. The family remembers. The caregiver remembers who showed and who didn't. Don't forget the caregivers.

We, as so many families and individuals, have experienced this first-hand. All I can say is it's hurtful to the person with dementia and it's hurtful for the family and caregivers. It creates bad feelings and is very hard to understand how people who had called themselves your friends or brothers and sisters in Christ can just stop the relationship cold. I read in posts where family members estrange themselves from the person with dementia also. We, for the most part, had family/relatives stand by us and support us and come and visit and call from Michigan when they could. We did experience a little family distance, but the immediate relationships/friendships that stopped cold were what affected us most. They missed out being with a wonderful man and showing him support. I think they missed what God would have wanted from them. Showing love is the main thing, showing love. All you can do is keep moving forward and continue with life without them. Concentrate on the people who are there for you and focus on them as God's gifts in your lives now. God was there for us the entire time; He never left, and that's what matters.

The biggest thing you can do is forgive and love those who have seemed to have forgotten about you. That's what Christ would do. They are not bad people, they just don't know how to cope with the situation at hand. That's what we have done—forgave. Carrying bitterness just makes you ill and isn't worth it. Forgive and carry on.

"There is life beyond diagnosis."

Harry Urban

CHAPTER 11

REVISITING DIAGNOSIS

Life shouldn't stop once you are diagnosed with a dementia-type disease or any disease. Life needs to go on and be lived to the fullest possible. We, as the family and caregivers, need to make sure life is as normal as possible and to stay active. Exercise is highly recommended for patients with Alzheimer's and won't hurt the caregivers either. Walking together gives you one-on-one time. Go to your loved one's favorite places. Try and do activities that make them happy. Get involved in what they can still do. Even living in the Alzheimer's World, make the best out of each day and live <u>on</u>.

2BeCourageous updated their status.
October 28, 2013 – 2:34 p.m.
Chet has been in Vanderbilt Hospital since Saturday. We are trying to nail down if he is having seizures, but the spells will not show themselves since we've been here. He had around eleven of them between Friday night and Saturday, but none after we got here. Grrrrr, you wicked and tricky

episodes of unknown causes. Nap time, it's not easy to rest in a hospital. Pray, if these are seizures, they show themselves while he is on the EEG.

2BeCourageous updated their status.
October 30, 2013 – 3:20 p.m.
We came home yesterday from the hospital, no episodes the entire time he was there. He has an appointment on November 6th at the Vanderbilt Neurology Clinic … trying to get his medical/psychological tests that Social Security Disability paid to have done because Vandy has requested them.

It amazes me and frustrates me at the same time how dementia and these spells are blamed on stress first before looking at other options. Stress can be so influential over our illnesses.

My son said to me a few weeks ago that he feels like his dad has skipped stages and is so much worse. He is always positive about his dad and how to handle these changes. This is the first I've seen frustration from him over it. Praying they will try Chet on a new medication for dementia and praying what we have seen in him are not seizures, for seizure medications are nasty to the body for some people. I've been on a few for depression and fibromyalgia, and I do not tolerate them well. I can't seem to wake up today, the living at the hospital burns you out.

Heidi DeBoer was at Paul Mitchell the School Murfreesboro.
November 12, 2013 – 8:19 a.m.
Today, my youngest child (by thirty minutes), Chesanne Daly DeBoer (Chessie DeBoer), graduates from Paul Mitchell School in Murfreesboro after starting her future professional career last December 12. She was invited into Phase 2, an optional advanced phase the school offers, with an average grade throughout the year of 99.36%. She now qualifies to take the state licensing exams in the next six weeks once her paperwork comes in to register. We are so proud of you, Chessie, and love you so very much.

2BeCourageous updated their status.
November 14, 2013 – 8:59 p.m.
The neurologist called today and has ordered a lumbar puncture on Chet, saying it will help determine what and what is not going on with him, so they can make a better plan for him. So, I told him and said it was up to him if he wants to go through this. He immediately got pouty mad and said it was torture being in the hospital. I said it would be an hour or so, he wasn't staying, and I told him it might hurt some. He said he was fine and doing good, so I had to remind him how the changes in the MRI alarmed the doctors. He didn't have any idea what I was talking about with the MRI.

So, since I was leaving it up to him, I called in Mr. Smooth Talker who knows what to say to his dad when I don't—my son, Jake (19). He gave it his best shot of encouraging him, then we dropped the subject. When I came home from being out a couple of hours, Chet said he decided to have it done if I thought he should. I hope I'm right in wanting this for him, knowing it will hurt some physically.

Heidi DeBoer updated her status.
November 19, 2013 – 11:28 p.m.
(Laughing) I'm sitting next to Braydon at dinner, and he has opted to eat his mac and cheese by the fistful. I'm holding his hand, wiping it off with a napkin and his nose is running, so he leans over and wipes his nose off on my hand and then wipes his mouth on my arm, (laughing). Chessie cracks up laughing as I'm sure the look on my face was "Ewwww." Hahaha

Speaking of runny noses, I asked in a support group if it was common for people with dementia to have their noses drip while they eat but not other times. Many people said that happens to their loved one too. I don't know why this happens, but Chet can't get through a meal without wiping his nose a dozen times. He was never like that before he got dementia.

2BeCourageous updated their status.
November 21, 2013 – 5:46 p.m.

We close on our house next Tuesday, the 26th. I'm feeling overwhelmed with packing again. We have moved four times in seven years. I give Chet jobs to do, and he gets so lost in some of them. Me, putting twenty knickknacks in front of him and a wet rag and two boxes and all the bath towels, then saying, "Clean all these off with this rag, then wrap them in the bath towels, then put them in the boxes, and tape them" seems simple enough. But not to a person with dementia. He needed me to say clean these, and that's it. Then, when he is done and accomplished that, then tell him to wrap them. When he is done wrapping them, then box them. ONE STEP AT A TIME! When am I going to get this? Ugh! He did fine when explained the right way for him to understand.

2BeCourageous updated their status.
December 09, 2013 – 10:54 a.m.

PRAYER FOR CHET … please pray for Chet today for he is having a lumbar puncture at 1:00 p.m. They are not sedating him and it's painful. I think they will numb the spine area, though, that part hurts too. The purpose is to be able to hopefully give a better idea of exact disease and figure out why it is progressing so fast. His brain MRI was very bad; a lot of shrinkage of gray matter.

2BeCourageous updated their status.
December 18, 2013 – 8:34 p.m.

Chet has another diagnosis, frontotemporal dementia. There are variations of this disease and he has a rarer form called logopenic progressive aphasia, it is a type of primary progressive aphasia. His Alzheimer's portion of his tests won't be back until after Christmas and, many times, the two will coincide. Not always but, considering the memory issues, I won't be surprised if he has both.

Logopenic progressive aphasia is on the left side of the brain in the frontal lobe and temporal lobe. The brain shrinks away and cells die is how I understand it. Again, I am not a doctor. The left side is where speech, spelling, writing, comprehension takes place. Chet cannot bring his words out correctly, he will say wrong words meant for other words, he cannot spell the words, he cannot form sentences at times, so will say, "Forget it" and give up. He also cannot comprehend language; if you give him instruction and say too long of a sentence, he can't work it out in his brain. Why? Those parts of his brain are disappearing. When he doesn't understand what I'm telling him, it's because he cannot process language like he once could. They finally showed us his latest MRI and the left side of his brain has many large black spaces where the brain has shrunk and brain cells have died. Seeing the MRI, for me, brought reality right in my face, better than anything about these horrid diseases has yet. I had all I could do to hold it together. They were handing me Kleenex. I fought the tears back, but now, tonight, the floodgates are starting to open.

He could become mute eventually, unable to communicate at all as he loses more of those parts of his brain. It's not like he will understand me and just can't respond; as the brain deteriorates, it will be impossible to understand us. Those parts will disappear. You can't ever fix that once it's gone. This could happen in two to five years. No one knows how long until he will no longer understand, could be longer. He will become more agitated and angry as time passes.

This diagnosis leaves the memory part up in the air, most likely a form of Alzheimer's is involved. What causes these things? The best answer is a combination of environmental and genetics. It doesn't mean past relatives had it or future will get it, but, somewhere in the genes, it lies. I was told today the specialist would have better details on all this after Christmas. The doctors told me there is no way I can do this alone, that I will need help to give me breaks during the days or week. I will need a support system. I responded, "Diseases like this make people fearful, I have read where friends and family have bowed out of patients' lives, fear does that. Not everyone can cope with this kind of thing." The doctor said that the other doctor helps spouses and family find support systems locally and day care centers.

I have a wonderful online support group, and my kids are here, the rest of family is in Michigan, and I can't write anymore because I'm losing it. I understand so much better after today, and it all makes sense.

2BeCourageous updated their status.
December 20, 2013 – 6:49 p.m.
I guess I was burned out. Went to bed last night about 11:30 p.m. to 12:00 midnight, woke up at 1:30 in the afternoon to the sound of a basketball game outside between Jake and Chet. Chet is smiling. Then they started a game of bocce in our yard, so I ate something and went back to bed until 4:30 p.m. when my son jumped on the bed and said, "So, what are you cooking for dinner?" (Laughing) Good grief, I never sleep into late morning even. Have felt under the weather since Wednesday night. It did my heart good to see Jake and Chet outside enjoying the day.

Heidi DeBoer updated her status.
December 24, 2013 – 6:14 p.m.
Had a wonderful Christmas Eve with Chet DeBoer, Jake DeBoer, Chessie DeBoer, Braydon Plung, and Brandon Plung. Good dinner and even s'mores from the fireplace. Love you all. Looking forward to Christmas dinner at the Plung's house (Brandon's parents' house). God is so good. We did our tradition of singing "Happy Birthday" to Jesus, this year with cheesecake and a candle. Jesus is what this holiday is all about. Celebrate Him.

2BeCourageous updated their status.
January 05, 2014 – 2:50 a.m.
I was gone Saturday from 9–6, shopping wedding dresses with my daughter, Chessie, and her future mother-in-law, Kim. Jake, my son, was home all day with Chet. I got home and received a welcome from my husband of "There you are, finally!" in a tone that said, "I'm happy to see you, thank God, you're home!" A while later, he says to me, "Did you see all

that I did?" I looked at the living room and kitchen that I left clean, and it looked clean!

I said, "Oh, it looks great in here! Thank you." He just looked at me. I asked, "Wrong answer?"

He said, "Follow me," very proudly to our bedroom that was also the way it was when I left. I stood there stumped until I noticed he had taken all the framed photos I had not hung yet, about ten to twelve of them, and stood them upright on the floor lining the wall. He said, "Look what I did."

I said, "I see."

He pointed to each one and said, "That's you, and there I am, and that one is me, not sure we need two, and there is Jake, and that's Chessie." As he went on, I stared at him with his child-like manner, no longer hearing him and my stomach turning into knots. I wasn't sure what he was doing. Perhaps reassuring himself or me that he knew who the people were in the photos, or reassuring me he still had value.

I don't have a punchline for everything I write, though I try to incorporate humor a lot in our lives and viewpoints. Today, I found none but thought it was sweet. I smiled and said, "I'll need your help hanging those this week, you're better than I at that."

He said, "Oh good, I'll help you!"

2BeCourageous updated their status.
January 10, 2014 – 8:52 p.m.
Chet met his new neurologist today at Vanderbilt. She was very nice; I really liked her. So, what it comes down to is the only way you know for sure for 100% accurate diagnosis of what causes dementia is an autopsy. I'm not quite wanting to sign him up for that yet to find out what has caused him this, and Chet said he does have his limits! Ha!

With that said, the blood test was back to show the range where you fall on getting Alzheimer's; his came back with an average chance of getting the disease. I thought it would be more technical than small, average, or high. So, the spinal fluid testing did imply Alzheimer's was a high probability. I have no idea why, but it did.

The doctor feels he has Alzheimer's with logopenic progressive aphasia. She isn't sure if the logopenic progressive aphasia's (the language comprehension and speech problem) origin is from frontotemporal dementia or the Alzheimer's advancing into that region of the brain. She showed me where Alzheimer's starts in the brain. I said, "The other doctors at the last visit said it was his left side of the brain that is the wiring for language. I was under the impression it wasn't bad on the right."

She said, "No it's on both sides, they were showing you why the language and comprehension were so bad, it's bad on both sides."

Sigh.

She won't change his medication of Aricept that his PCP started him on last year because they just increased it (doubled from 10 mg to 20 mg) and it's only been six weeks or so, and she wants to give it two more months. Then, she will consider Namenda with the Aricept. She said there are no pills for the aphasia and has referred him to speech pathology. I asked what he can gain from that. She said, "They will help with giving him ways to communicate better, and giving us ways to get things across to him better. It may be picture boards for example." What it all comes down to is it is what it is, even if we're not sure of the exact cause. It is what it is, and it's not going away, and it's not going to get better, but, through God, we will endure because love wins.

2BeCourageous updated their status.
January 11, 2014 – 6:16 p.m.
Today, I asked Chet to please bring me the dirty laundry hamper from our bedroom. He stared at me. So, I said, "The dirty laundry in the hamper where you throw your dirty clothes."

He asked, "What's a hamper?"

So, I calmly (See, calm is not my strong point, medication working once again!) walked him to the bedroom and lifted the lid and told him, "This is the hamper. Can you carry it to the laundry room for me?"

He said "Sure."

I left for the laundry room. He showed up a few minutes later empty handed. I asked, "Why didn't you bring it?

He said, "Bring what?"

I called Jake's name. Jake listening to the whole thing, I'm sure, waiting for me to blow and I did not, says, "I know the laundry hamper."

This is a family living in a world of dementia. I need to ask him to do things, he needs to have value, but I'm ever so learning how to cope when he doesn't get me. I still fail a lot. This is what the neurologist meant how a speech pathologist would be able to help us communicate better, for it will help win some battles in this war on dementia.

2BeCourageous updated their status.
January 12, 2014 – 9:16 p.m.
Well, we have cut back on sugar in our house, salt too. We now use half and half. Yup, half sugar and half salt. Being helpful, bless his heart, Chet took the sugar container on the stove and refilled the half empty salt shaker with it. Then got the salt refill container out and topped off the sugar container with it. He couldn't figure out why his green bean casserole tasted sweet after seasoning it in his bowl. It's never boring, I couldn't stop laughing at the table and so was Chet and Jake.

2BeCourageous updated their status.
February 01, 2014 – 1:00 a.m.
I have been sick for a week; it's unbelievable how much snot your head can hold (laughing). I have been getting up in the middle of the night because I feel worse lying down and can't breathe. Sitting in the recliner in the living room helps, and I fall asleep there until morning. (Ha, when we first got married, Chet wouldn't have a recliner because they were for old folks. We bought one with this last move; I'm an old folk now.)

We were watching a movie and Chet decided to head to bed at 8:30 p.m. before the movie was over. We said our good nights and I love yous, and, about ten minutes later, he comes back out upset and says to me, "Don't you like my bed anymore?"

Me: "What?"

Him: "I'm always alone in there, by myself!"

Me: "The movie isn't over yet, and it's only 8:30. I have been getting up at night because I can't breathe. I've felt so sick, so I sleep in the chair instead of bed bothering you."

Him: "The movie isn't over? Crap!"

Ha, so much for the concern on how I'm feeling.

I find this incident interesting because he sleeps all night but knows and remembers I'm not in there with him at some point. He mentioned the other day he woke up alone and didn't understand why. I had sensed concern from him other times when I was gone with my daughter, wedding shopping and we were gone several hours. When I got home, he said, "Where were you so long?!" It wasn't that he was alone, he wasn't, but I could sense fear in him. I've sensed this fear from him a few times now, like he might lose me somehow. I reassure him I'm not going anywhere, that I'm his, that he is stuck with me until the end of time. But I'm sensing I will be having to keep reassuring him in the future. The past him never showed fear or outward worry. This is another adjustment to our new normal.

2BeCourageous updated their status.
February 02, 2014 – 4:22 p.m.

A mentionable moment.

Sitting in the living room after dinner with my son Jake, watching *The Fast and the Furious*, an intense street race scene was on. Chet was doing dishes and our focus is on the TV. We hear Chet now yelling loudly standing in the living room.

Chet yelling: "DOES NO ONE EVEN CARE THAT I'M BLEEDING?!"

Jake and I turn to look at the same time, startled.

Me: "What? What happened?" (As I quickly get up to look.)

Chet: (holding his finger out) "I kept saying I'm BLEEDING several times and no one came. I could have bled to death!"

Me: (now smiling) "Aww, show me, I don't see blood."

Chet: (looking for the cut) "Right here!"

Me: "That's a paper cut, I think you'll live!"

Chet: "It still bled!"

Me: "I'm sorry, I didn't hear you (hugging him), but I was watching Paul Walker, his hotness must have turned my hearing off!"

Chet snaps the dish towel at me and laughs at me.

I always try to make him laugh if I can. Such drama!

2BeCourageous updated their status.
February 08, 2014 – 2:23 a.m.

I so don't understand these diseases! The last week my husband has struggled very little with speech. He is using the correct words, not hesitating, searching for words, more joking also. He has been picking on me in a fun way.

Language comprehension is the same, meaning it doesn't all connect smoothly when you ask or give instruction. Tomorrow he may go back to saying wrong words or lost for words. How can it turn on and off? Tricks these diseases play.

"But the fruit of the Spirit is love, joy, peace, patience, kindness, goodness, faithfulness, gentleness, self-control; against such things there is no law."

GALATIANS 5:22–23 NASB

CHAPTER 12

SPEECH THERAPY

2BeCourageous
March 01, 2014 – 12:31 a.m.

It's been a tough week, Chet and I are both sick for two weeks now, and this took him from highly improved in speech and attitude and humor to five steps backward, having trouble talking and confused. We both went on antibiotics, steroids, and cough medicine, with me getting a bonus of an antibiotic shot in the hip to kick-start me. Prayer, please, that we feel better soon.

Just a note that steroids mess with diabetes levels, plus they made Chet hyper and agitated, and he paced a lot while on them.

2BeCourageous updated their status.
Mar 01, 2014 – 12:40 a.m.

Day one—coconut oil capsules 1000 mg, two [capsules] two times a day is the dose. I started Chet on half that. Just two capsules. I will repeat tomorrow, then, Sunday, add one more capsule. By Wednesday, he will be on four a day. We'll reevaluate in two weeks if I increase it by one. I don't want to try the cumin pills at the same time as this. We will give this three months. Pray and wish us luck.

****

There are so many over the counter treatments and claims to cure Alzheimer's, coconut oil being one of them, cumin, marijuana, one doctor told us blueberries brought back some cognitive function in his father, and the list goes on. If it sounds too good to be true, it probably is. At the same time, it's so easy to get caught up in all the hype over new cure claims because you desperately want it to be true. There are just as many causes out there on what causes Alzheimer's. Being overweight, diabetes, high cholesterol, environmental toxins, diet, deficiencies in vitamin D. It seems there's a new reason or cause every day on the Internet. In my mind, if they knew why it happened, couldn't they then cure it? I question everything now and don't jump on the bandwagon of new cures. One day, somebody will be right, but it will make front story news because this disease will affect everyone in some way before their life is over. You will know someone, if not in your own family, going through this, then in someone else's family that you know. I'm trying the coconut oil, desperate for something to work and help him.

2BeCourageous updated their status.
March 11, 2014 – 9:07 p.m.
Chet had his follow-up appointment at Vanderbilt today. I like his doctor, she explains things well and takes time. She asked Chet why he was here, he had no idea and seemed put out by the fact that he had to come. She asked him if he knew what he had, he did not. Sigh.

She asked him if he had any problems with his memory or with his speech. He said, "Not that I'm aware of." Double sigh. He did not know his birth date, and I never know when the nurse asks him all these questions before the doctor comes in like birth date, address if it's a test, or should I answer for him? So, I say, "Should I answer?"

The doctor asked me, "Do you understand what he has?"

I said, "Early-onset Alzheimer's and frontotemporal dementia has been discussed." She reminded me there is no absolute diagnosis until death and autopsy. But she feels strongly he has logopenic variant primary progressive aphasia related to Alzheimer's disease. A mouthful, huh? She talked me into getting him seen by speech and language pathology, to be tested to see if there is help with communication skills. I put it off last time; now, I will follow through.

Chet has been on Aricept 10 mg for a long time now, well, over a year and on 20 mg for about three to four months. She is adding Namenda; I asked her if he is staying on the Aricept. She told me he would be on it the rest of his life for they have done studies that show being taken off it causes quicker decline, or the patient does worse. The Namenda is not meant to improve memory, though some have experienced that; it's meant to delay brain cell death, so it doesn't happen as fast. She has never had a patient have a bad reaction to it.

I told her I put Chet on coconut oil capsules; she asked what I knew about it. I said, "To feed the brain." She said, since we were discussing brain food, she told me about a powder that you mix with water and drink; I can't remember the name, dang it. It's classified food type to feed the brain, and there have been many good results with it on Alzheimer's patients. Again, she doesn't want to throw too many new things at once, so he hasn't been on the coconut oil long enough to see any difference yet. Adding the Namenda is a gradual dose increase thing, so the powder drink is on hold. Insurance does not pay for it and it's outrageous in price. Something we can't afford.

2BeCourageous updated their status.
March 12, 2014 – 9:25 a.m.

While sitting waiting for my doctor yesterday (after Chet's doctor appointment), I was making conversation with him, and I said, "You know, your baby girl is getting married in one month."

He said, "Really?"

I said, "Yes, and you are walking her down the aisle."

His eyes opened big and he looked at me now beaming and said, "I am?"

I said, "Of course, you're her daddy and fathers walk their daughters down the aisle; you will give her away to Brandon."

He is beaming proud with a smile and says, "I'm part of it?"

Me: "Yup, you have to get fitted for a suit to rent."

Chet: "Wow!"

Me: "Our friend, Danny, wrote a song for a father-daughter dance, and he is going to sing it while you dance with Chessie!"

This made Chet's day; I loved the look on his face.

Love this man; making memories.

Brandon is Chesanne's high school sweetheart since tenth grade. They will be getting married on April 12th, 2014. Chesanne went to cosmetology school and has her license now. Brandon works in his dad's motorcycle shop, repairing bikes.

2BeCourageous updated their status.
March 16, 2014 – 3:51 p.m.

Watching *Americas Funniest Videos* with Chet. It's something I can put on TV, and it always changes his mood to happy. He laughs and laughs, so do I. It never gets old watching people hurt themselves. (Laughing)

2BeCourageous updated their status.
March 19, 2014 – 10:14 p.m.

Today Chet had an appointment back at Vanderbilt (wonderful medical center), this time, in their Speech and Language Rehabilitation Center for an evaluation. It was pretty much determined that, when shown photos of items, he would look lost like he didn't recognize it, though he really did recognize it. Say, like a picture of a "tennis racket," he couldn't tell her what it was when, in fact, he did recognize it, but his memory for the word wasn't connecting to it. He did the motion of swinging it and said "net." So, instead of asking him to tell them what was in the photo after a few fails, they gave him options. Picture of a banana; he couldn't come up with the word, so they asked, "Is this an orange or a banana?" Well then, he could say banana.

Using too many words in giving directions to ask him to do something, he is totally lost. He couldn't follow the direction. I told them I'd realized that already at home; for example, if I say, "Will you go to the laundry room and take out the clothes in the dryer and fold them?" He can't do this. He starts to walk and stops and says, "What am I supposed to do?" I must make it one step at a time.

The psychologist suggested that I have the directions written out in the laundry room in steps for him. Me saying, "Will you go into the laundry room for me?" is step 1, so when he gets there, I can say or he can read on his own: step 2) Chet takes laundry out of the dryer, Step 3) fold it. She also suggested to have a schedule for him on a calendar: take your pills, eat breakfast, shower, play basketball, go for walk with Heidi, rake the leaves. Have it all scheduled each day so he can read it, do it so he can feel independent as long as he can. So he can do things and feel value and not be so horribly bored. Give him projects. Let him do as much as he can be trusted with on his own.

Things he can't do on his own is cook. But he can help me, and I should let him help me. She wants us to have a big calendar up and, each day, put the day of the week up, the date up, and the month up like they do in grade schools. Then write the day's events on each day. So he doesn't have to wonder constantly what day or month it is ten times a day. We go back in a month or so to figure out picture boards and ask me for use farther down the road when communication becomes a bigger struggle. We aren't to the point of needing those yet. Much of their testing, they couldn't do because he didn't understand it.

This, my friends, is what's called living in the Alzheimer's World.

2BeCourageous updated their status.
March 21, 2014 – 8:46 a.m.

I don't know how to stay on top of my game and grieve at the same time. I know I have been grieving on and off, but it can take you into the depths of despair. Being one with a past of depression problems, I can't risk that for I need to be everyone's superhero, but my cape is torn and it's hard to fly some days. Sigh.

2BeCourageous updated their status.
March 23, 2014 – 10:42 p.m.

I got some mini chalkboards to start implementing the plans discussed during the speech evaluation. He took his morning medications without me reminding him, and this medication sign on the chalkboard helps me remember to check his and my own. The date board I set off to the side of the TV stand. He liked that; you can get all kinds of chalkboards at Hobby Lobby or make your own with chalkboard paint.

I also ordered for him from Shutterfly luggage tags with his photo on it and name and address and phone numbers, and saying he has Alzheimer's and to call his family. He can keep these in his pocket or wear it around his neck when we go out. The luggage tags were more durable than a business type card on paper.

2BeCourageous updated their status.
March 24, 2014 – 11:48 p.m.

Not the best day on my part. I was sarcastic and mean-spirited not only to my husband but my daughter as well, and I became frustrated with my grandson while he was playing with my Kindle and wouldn't let me put the charger in it while he was sitting on me. It was the battle of the wills. He won (me laughing), he put both hands on my face and kissed me; how can you stay mad after that? Leave it to a two-year-old to make things better.

I know it sounds like I am mad and angry all the time, but there are good days too, well, as good as it can get living in the Alzheimer's World.

I just seemed to have written more in my blog about the bad or noticeable days, and there are always lessons on those bad days. Some dates are a month apart, and a lot happens in between the days I write. I can't put it all in this book, and it can get hard finding the good from these diseases. There just isn't any good that comes naturally; you must work at it in the later stages, you have to put effort into making their world better. The caregiver has the loved one's life in their hands. The caregiver has a lot of responsibility put on them, that's why they need support from others, even if it's just "You are doing an amazing job," they need to hear something good and be surrounded by friends and family.

"Be completely humble and gentle; be patient, bearing with one another in love."

EPHESIANS 4:2 NIV

CHAPTER 13

HERE COMES THE BRIDE

2BeCourageous updated their status.
March 29, 2014 – 11:24 a.m.

Well, Chet's been very active and helpful around the house. He folded and put away and hung on hangers two weeks of dirty laundry in our closet and drawers. He took a pile of important papers and decided what should be kept and what should be tossed. He tossed my bills and some house documents.

After I'm not sure how long, a couple days, I had to convince him to change his clothes. That has never been an issue until the last month or so. He changed his clothes almost daily. I woke up the other night to him waking up startled, then putting his cap and glasses on and going back to sleep. I got him to take his glasses back off. Cap stayed on.

I'm not feeling well today, fibro flair most likely from this weather has me down. Feeling overwhelmed, wedding two weeks away, ahhhhh! Excited, just need to feel better. Did terrible on the budget, spending too much on the wedding left me with $38 until next Thursday. We will survive this. God gets us through always. Just venting today.

2BeCourageous updated their status.
March 30, 2014 – 9:06 p.m.
Being a caregiver to someone with dementia can cause a lot of stress and depression, especially if the caregiver is doing it alone. Respite, meaning a break away from being a caregiver, can help a lot; even a couple of hours helps. Some nursing facilities have respite beds, and your loved one can stay for so many days to a couple of weeks, so that the caregiver can have a refreshing break. Friends and family are so important to the caregiver in giving them the support and breaks needed to keep them going.

2BeCourageous updated their status.
April 03, 2014 – 10:34 p.m.
Wow! Very bad day for Chet's clarity, gee whiz. I have decided for sure now to require name tags for all guests next week, from family coming in early for the wedding and at the rehearsal and the wedding.

Chessie, my daughter, is getting married April 12th, and she had over to our house today her two bridesmaids, so they could try on their dresses. One's boyfriend also came with her. Chet asked me at least eight times what their names were, and asked several times how Chessie knew them, and asked several times where the wedding was going to be. They were here about an hour. Chet realized he wasn't remembering, I told him about the name tag idea and he liked it. This throws me off because, yesterday, he had so much clarity and understanding on everything. Oh, Alzheimer's, I so don't get you.

The chalkboards are working great for the most part, especially when I remember to put the correct day of the week on it (laughing). Yikes! I have added a mini chalkboard next to the date and day board on the TV stand that says, "Chessie's Wedding … 9 more days … April 12" (I change the number daily). He said today, "Nine more days until the wedding!" He sees this as he watches TV. Success!

2BeCourageous updated their status.
April 07, 2014 – 11:05 p.m.
With a little wedding stress building, I was easily agitated today, plus my dinner was not starting out well. My temper was getting shorter as my fried potatoes were a mess, sticking to the pan. I was tired and in pain, along with having to give Chet direction over and over on the same topic. I said in a sarcastic tone to my daughter who was making wedding decorations at the table, "This is going to be such a long life!"

She says without missing a beat, "Well, Mom, it shouldn't be that long; yours is more than half over already!" Smart-alecky girl child! Hahaha, she made me laugh!

2BeCourageous updated their status.
April 12, 2014 – 10:48 a.m.
Chet is walking his baby girl down the aisle today; he is so excited! He had his tux on at 8:00 a.m. Jake had him take it off since the wedding is at 5:30 p.m. It's going to be a good day!

Update: It was such a wonderful day. Chessie looked beautiful and my dream of seeing Chet walk his baby girl down the aisle came true. I was so proud of him. He looked so handsome and he was so happy with a grin on his face the entire day. He did the father-daughter dance and I had happy tears. I could not have asked for a better, happier day. A lot of families came down from Michigan, which made it extra special.

2BeCourageous updated their status.
April 29, 2014 – 7:34 p.m.
I felt heartbroken yesterday. My mom (89), called to talk and then put my ten-years-older-than-I sister, Sandy, on so that we could chat. One of Chet's concerns over that last few years is what will happen to Sandy when my mom passes. We have no family left on my mom's side and Sandy's dad's side, she never knew. (We have different dads). She turns sixty-seven in June and there would be no one for her in Michigan. Chet

and I agreed she can live with us if she so decides she can't make it on her own. Who can on just Social Security retirement?

So, anyway, I hang up from talking to her and Chet asks, "Who was that?"

I said, "Sandy."

He says, "Sandy? Sandy …. Who is Sandy?"

I said, "My sister."

He says, "Oh really?"

These kinds of conversations break my heart. He has been more confused this week. But when I asked him today about Sandy, if he knew who she was, he said he did.

2BeCourageous updated their status.
May 03, 2014 – 12:07 a.m.

Went to Walmart today with Chet, Weed Eater shopping. We are back in the garden center, I'm reading all the Weed Eater boxes and he walks around to the next aisle, so I follow him and tell him I'm not finished in the aisle I was in.

He said, "I want to be in this aisle I'm in."

"Fine," I said. "But do not leave and I'm one over."

He snaps "I'm not leaving!"

So, a few minutes later, I go to get him to give input on the one I wanted. He is gone, nowhere in home and garden. Nervously, I'm calling his name and I finally see him way the heck up at the front cash registers talking to a worker. I'm waving to him like a mad woman in hopes he sees me and the guy doesn't get on the intercom. I know, if he is flustered, his words don't go together well, so I do not know what he told the guy. Just in time, he saw me; I asked him why he left, he said to find me and had to get someone to help search for me. If I treat him like he isn't capable, he gets mad and pouts, but every time, lately, I give him the lead way, he messes up. My medication must have been on overtime because I didn't get mad at him, I followed that old saying: "Keep calm and live in the dementia world!"

2BeCourageous updated their status.
May 04, 2014 – 7:42 p.m.

God bless my son, Jake, he is in the kitchen explaining to Chet how to warm up leftover taco meat from earlier today and what to put in the bowl for taco salad. Each separate step. Chet had no clue; he used to be the main cook. The things we take for granted in knowing how to do is slowly lost before our eyes and changed forever. Dementia changing us all in different ways.

2BeCourageous updated their status.
May 15, 2014 – 10:04 p.m.

Talking about the wedding today, Chet said proudly, "I remember that day, I remember every bit of it, it was a wonderful, wonderful day!" My heart is still smiling from hearing him say that! I wanted so bad for him to have that moment and memory with his baby girl and one month later, he is still delighted with the memories of the day. I love his smile and the glow that day captured in pictures. I love him so much!

2BeCourageous updated their status.
May 25, 2014 – 12:53 a.m.

Well, so far, our Memorial Day weekend has been great! Chet's sister, Sue, and his other sister, Joyce, came from Michigan to visit us. Chet is so pleased to see them. Chet even sat through a game of "What's Yours Like?" It is a question-and-answer type game and, even though he didn't always understand it, he didn't get frustrated and laughed a lot, which is a common occurrence when we are with his family. They are a feel-good, silly in a fun way, laugh-until-your-side-hurts type of family. It does my heart good to see their love and understanding for Chet, especially when I've read in support groups how for some people with dementia, their family members don't want to be around them, visiting, calling, or helping. That's so sad. We are blessed with a loving family.

We have, though, experienced that, with some people here whom we thought were very close good friends since the first month we moved here seven years ago until Chet became ill. It was like a wall came down and their heart now seems cold. It is so hurtful to have that done when my husband needed to know he had friends that would stand by him while he goes on this journey. I flat out tell people, Alzheimer's is NOT contagious! I know there is a stigma and a fear factor for both sides, but knowing that doesn't make it hurt less. We forgive but don't always forget. Thank God, we are blessed with a family that loves us and drives 600 miles for short weekend visits to see us when they can. Laughter is the best medcine; we are filling up on it this weekend.

2BeCourageous updated their status.
June 06, 2014 – 9:09 a.m.
I should be thrilled my husband wants to help with dishes, but he is doing them with dirty rags; not washing a plate, just wiping it off and washing coffee cups in the bathroom with toilet paper. I'm just not thrilled, though, don't ask me why, just not! Feeling frustrated. I redid them after he went to bed, did not make a scene. I know, I'm learning!

2BeCourageous updated their status.
June 09, 2014 – 8:25 p.m.
Chet and I are lightning bug watching, and I always feel amazed by them. They make the world enchanted and for a bit, you can escape reality watching them. We used to walk around on the farm in the moonlight and fog, watching the lightning bugs. The horses walking around with us just barely seeing them in the mist and the little light tails of the bugs blinking all through the pasture. It was so magical holding hands with my husband and watching the lights twinkle.

Speaking of light, one thing I try to do for Chet and myself is have bright light in the house. I make sure all the blinds on the windows are open, so daylight comes in and I use lamps also to create more light during the day. Light treatment has been used to treat winter depression; I try to get Chet out in the sunlight as much as we can. Light has been shown in studies to improve depression, agitation, and promote better sleep at night. It's so worth a try.

Update: The coconut oil capsules have not made any difference in Chet, and, due to cost and no improvement, I am stopping them. We tried for a few months and he has shown decline more than improvement. You just have that hope because someone out there said it works, it will cure them. I wanted to believe so much, but nothing is going to cure him.

2BeCourageous updated their status.
June 22, 2014 – 8:25 p.m.
Chet has taken to our new puppy, Snow. We have a shih tzu named Maggie and she is eleven years old. I thought it was time to bring in a new dog since Maggie is on the end side of her life cycle. Snow is half lab and half rat terrier. Chet had bad feelings about getting a new dog. Until he saw six-week-old Snow, Jon Snow. We let Chet hold him on the way home, and I think he liked that puppy!

Being a caregiver to someone with Alzheimer's is very challenging and can wear you down quickly. You need to consider yourself and find ways to take breaks. You need to live in the real world also. Your loved one is no longer the same person, their entire way of thinking changes; calm, mild-mannered may now be very difficult and can turn irrational and make no sense. We, as caregivers, need to learn how to live in your loved one's world for the world we shared no longer makes sense to them. But, for our sanity's sake, we need to be with healthy thinking people also. Find time for yourself, ask a friend to sit with your loved one, and go out and get away for a bit. I repeat this because I can't stress it enough.

I get annoyed by videos, which make Alzheimer's sound like it's just a senior/elderly disease and it's not at all! My husband was diagnosed at fifty-seven, but we tried for a couple of years to figure it out. I read that the disease can be starting with no symptoms ten to twenty years before diagnosis. I have met online people from age twelve, eighteen, others in their thirties and upward that have dementia. It's is no longer an elderly disease. My grandfather and great grandmother had a dementia disease but after age sixty-five. Chet's grandparents had a dementia type disease also but not until their late eighties or early nineties. I had no idea people got these diseases at younger ages; I was shocked how many people I met online that have the younger onset, or I heard about them from their caregivers.

2BeCourageous updated their status.
July 12, 2014 – 9:55 p.m.
I keep a spray bottle of Dawn dish soap mixed with water to kill bugs with. I had taken the sprayer off to refill and I got side tracked. Next we know, the two-liter bottle of Coke, half full now, has the spray cap on it which had soap in the tube and nozzle, so ruined pop. Hmmm, the only person drinking Coke at the time saw nothing wrong with this and did not understand the fuss. I won't mention his name, but it wasn't my two-year-old grandson!

My husband seems frailer to me lately. I've been fighting depression, I'm doing this all wrong, I'm trying to live as normal as possible, and there isn't anything normal about this. I just prefer to hide and not go anywhere. I can't even make myself go to church; it's been months. I have social anxiety, and it's easy to talk myself out of going out to places. I hurt emotionally but try to ignore it. I need to get involved in life; I need to get him involved in life while he still can, my patience is so thin for everyone at times. My humor is my lifeline, so, when I'm not being funny, I'm in trouble. I just needed to vent. Humor can also cover the pain.

Why should a soapy spray cap on the Coke bottle wear on me? It otherwise would be humorous, but it was just another sting of reality that shows my best friend and husband has again stepped farther away from me. It's constant changes and we need to accept each change to move on, but then you need to grieve each change to accept it and let go of what was.

2BeCourageous updated their status.
July 17, 2014 – 12:39 a.m.
Chet and I sitting under our shade tree in the backyard, this was our conversation:

> Me: "Honey how do you feel you are doing?"
> Chet: "About what?"
> Me: "With your illness?"
> Chet: "I feel great, not sick."
> Me: "No, I mean with your Alzheimer's; you know you have it, right?"
> Chet: "Not really, I have no problems, I feel good."
> Me: "That's good, I'm glad things are good."
> Me: "Any concerns?"
> Chet: "Michigan, Michigan."
> Me: "I'm working that out."
> Me: "Well, okay then, I'm happy you are doing good … I love you."
> Chet: "I know, I love you too."

His language skills and understanding are rapidly declining; we are at the point I feel I can't leave him home alone anymore, he panics when he can't find us in the house and we are just in the backyard. He angers more quickly (I would too if I was in his place). Outdoor games we can engage him in, but he gets so mad if he misses or messes up. Well, okay, that one has always been normal for him (laughing). Name recognition of friends is not there, he does not remember them unless I go into detail or show him a photo, and, even then, he may not remember.

I will no longer tell him he has this dreaded disease. If he brings it up, fine, but I've decided there is nothing wrong if he wants to believe he is fine and that makes him feel better about himself, then, right now, we will go with it. He is very brave and handles his illness with class and dignity. Is he in denial? Who am I to say? His mind has decided to handle it this way, and I'm proud of him and love him so much.

Buying this house on an acre was the right move. He loves it outside in the backyard. He loves to putts and enjoys sitting under the big shade tree. He and Jake dug a hole and packed it smooth to make a putting green. Next will be a Frisbee Golf range; we have bocce and ladder golf and a basketball court, so we can stay busy outside. I just need to keep him busy. He sleeps great and I know this is huge. Praise! I'm rambling here and it's late, thanks for reading my stuff.

2BeCourageous updated their status.
July 17, 2014 – 7:22 p.m.
Today we went swimming at my daughter Chesanne's house (they live with Brandon's—my son in law—parents). It was so nice to get out and have a change of scenery and Chet enjoyed it. It was nice seeing him smile.

2BeCourageous updated their status.
July 20, 2014 – 9:59 a.m.
Happy 23rd anniversary, Chet, I love you much! He and I went out to dinner.

*"Be strong and of good courage, do not fear nor be afraid of them;
for the LORD your God, He is the One who goes with you. He will
not leave you nor forsake you."*

DEUTERONOMY 31:6 NKJV

CHAPTER 14

MUSIC TO MY EARS

" Did you know that people with Alzheimer's and other dementias can often remember songs and music long after their recollections of other things has faded away? It's true! Chet's favorite music is gospel music, and he can sing all the words to the songs he knows. He can pronounce them correctly and is in tune, it's amazing."

2BeCourageous updated their status.
July 26, 2014 – 8:59 p.m.
I was getting my Mariah Carey on, you know, trying for the high note when I turned around and saw Chet in bed with his eyes squeezed shut and his fingers in his ears. Hahaha, I'm sure it's his sensitivity to loud sound and not my singing.

2BeCourageous updated their status.
August 14, 2014 – 11:26 p.m.

I test very low on vitamin D and was taking D3 5000 daily, cheaper than the prescription kind but ran out a month ago and couldn't afford it. Sunshine and vitamin D from here on out! Going to have Chet's D level checked. In fact, I'll look online right now. All his labs are always posted at Vanderbilt. There is an article that says vitamin D deficiency more than doubles the risk of Alzheimer's dementia. Chet's D is low, so I will be putting him on D3 daily—why weren't we told about this? When my D levels get too low, I have more pain, I have noticed.

2BeCourageous updated their status.
August 26, 2014 – 9:13 p.m.

What a tense day. Four adults in the house today and a two-year-old, and the only happy one was the two-year-old! Our bad moods fed off each other. So, to lighten things up, we head to the park to practice softball for Jake, but being ninety degrees on the field did not help anyone's mood, except my grandson ran the entire time and had a great time laughing; give me that energy Lord! Praying for a less moody tomorrow!

2BeCourageous updated their status.
September 06, 2014 – 1:20 a.m.

I find myself questioning all my husband's moves lately. I think out of fear that a new stage is developing. Knowing from others who have these diseases in my support groups, or from caregivers, I know what to expect as far as stages or behaviors. So, when I see Chet, for example, three nights in a row restless and up and down, I get very nervous that sundowning may be starting. He is agitated lately. I would be too. No, wait, I'm am too. I know we feed off each other's emotions. I'm not sure how many times I have gotten up to go to the bathroom at night and come back to bed and have the bed made. (Laughing)

I asked Chet to pick out jigsaw puzzles, which he used to love. I found LARGE 300-piece puzzles at Rite Aid, but he refused, wasn't interested.

He wouldn't try Uno that I bought, but he says he is bored. He loves DVDs that he can watch that are Christian gospel with the Gaither Vocal Band, The Booth Brothers, Allison Kraus. So, I'm hoping I will be able to get these to give him something to watch and sing with; they are his favorites. I think I get agitated because the changes scare me. I'm scared.

2BeCourageous updated their status.
September 09, 2014 – 11:37 p.m.
I'm not sure if the dementia drugs like Aricept and Namenda are helping Chet or not. His decline is so fast. Are they causing more harm than good? One of the biggest complaints I read over and over is urinary tract infections (UTI) in dementia patients. If you look up Aricept and Namenda, the most common used dementia drugs, they can cause urinary retention. Wouldn't that explain so many UTIs? Chet has had several UTIs.

2BeCourageous updated their status.
September 18, 2014 – 10:44 p.m.
Been a good week, I think I'm catching on with the patience thing, well this week anyway. (End of post.)

****

I was having trouble accepting the person my husband was turning into. I yearned for my old Chet, the guy I married and fell in love with. I didn't want to let go of that guy. He was my everything! But he was getting farther and farther away. I adored my husband and, if I would let go of the old him, I was afraid I wouldn't adore him as I had in the past. Did I have to let go of the old him to accept the new man in my house? He kept changing. When I thought I could accept who he was, he changed even more. It was hard to keep up. The old him was not coming back to me; I had to accept the new person he kept changing into. I loved him and made a vow to stay by him. I could never abandon him; I promised him I'd keep him home. That wouldn't change.

2BeCourageous updated their status.

October 09, 2014 – 9:23 p.m.

Today, our conversation went like this:

Me: "Chet do you remember your job you left at the high school as a custodian?"

Chet: (long pause) "No."

Me: "Remember, you left it in December of 2012?"

Chet: "No, I don't."

Me: "Do you remember working at Lowes before the custodian job?"

Chet: "I think so, well, no."

Me: "Do you know why we moved to Tennessee end of 2006?"

Chet: "Why?"

Me: "Because you closed your business, Creative Retail Services, and went to work for one of your competitors here in Nashville doing Christian bookstore design and installations. Does that sound familiar?"

Chet: (shaking his head) "No."

Me: "They let you go eighteen months later because they didn't have enough work but waited so you could collect unemployment."

Chet: "Really?"

Me: "Do you remember your business in Michigan?"

Chet: "No."

Me: "That's okay, just making conversation."

Me: "Can you tell me about your brothers and sisters? Like, their names?"

Chet: "Well, sure. There's Joyce ... (long pause)."

Me: "You have two brothers and three sisters."

Chet: "Yes ... um, help me."

Me: "Joyce, Peg, Sue, Andy, and Phil."

Chet: "I would know if I saw pictures!"

Me: "I know, we will start making albums this weekend. Do you remember how beautiful our wedding was? We have tons of pictures."

Chet: "I don't.":(

Me: "Do you know that I love you?"
Chet: "Oh, I know that! I love you too."

One of the rules in the Alzheimer's World is not to ask "Do you remember?" FAIL!

Well, if you haven't figured out by now, these rules are easier said than done. For me anyway. If I don't ask these things, I have no idea where he is at because he hardly talks. It's not a regular occurrence I drill him. But I do ask him if he can remember, so I know what time frames are missing, so I can tell his doctor. Not remembering his jobs and not remembering our wedding and his family's names is huge to me, and shows me this disease process is going way to fast and the doctors can't tell me why. Some people with dementia from early-onset Alzheimer's seem not to advance like my husband has. Their verbal skills do not seem to be affected, and they can go out and talk at events about Dementia Awareness. Why has my husband's been rare and aggressive? We will never know. Charts give him five to ten years from diagnosis.

2BeCourageous updated their status.
November 21, 2014 – 7:49 p.m.

I took Chet with me to get my new glasses and then to my doctor's appointment at Vanderbilt Neurology at 100 Oaks, not as far as going to the hospital like we usually drive. You would have thought we were on the road for hours; he could not believe how far we went and how long we were gone. He complained about killing time in the shops at 100 Oaks. He complained about waiting in the waiting room for the doctor. Driving to Michigan is going to be torture. (Laughing—ahhhhhh, no I'm not!)

2BeCourageous updated their status.
December 03, 2014 – 10:32 p.m.

Last night, I surprised Chet and took him to see Brian Free and Assurance, the southern gospel quartet, in concert. They were in La Vergne and he loves them. They were at Miracle Baptist Church, and the Pastor had the audience sing an old Baptist hymn before the quartet took the stage. Chet (raised Baptist) sang every word without looking and no mistakes. He cannot say a whole sentence and after the third or fourth word, he is lost on what he wanted to say; wrong words come out; or he gives up and says, "Forget it!" His language skills are leaving him fast! Chet even sang along on some of the concert songs. I got out all our Brian Free and Assurance CDs we own today and all the other gospel CDs and played them for him today.

I have been following the making of the documentary *Alive Inside*. It was an experiment to see what digital music through iPods with headphones did for dementia and brain-injured patients. People that showed no recognition of their surroundings came alive when the headphones went on with music picked especially from their past. It's mind-blowing the difference it made.

2BeCourageous shared a link.
December 05, 2014 – 1:23 p.m.

I read an article about predicting Alzheimer's with blood tests, and I'm not sure if I'd want to know if I was going to get it if they can't do anything about it. So, if you know you're doomed with Alzheimer's, your mind plays the psychological card early on and performs as a doomed subject. But the fact is memory is affected ten to twenty years before diagnosis, not in major ways but it is affected. Hindsight is 20/20. Chet complained of memory problems in the late '90s, but we blamed it on a pesticide poisoning in our house. Will we ever know? No. Is this blood test good? Only for subjects willing to be tested on for new drugs is my opinion. Everyday Joe? No! Because autopsy results have shown people had the plaque and tangles caused by Alzheimer's and never had any symptoms of the disease. So, those people would have carried a major stress and worry and self-doubt with them, and they would have never had the active disease. Plus, there is no cure, there are no solid facts what causes it. How would it help to know ahead of time when modern medicine can't lessen it or cure it? I guess it gives you time to prepare and have things in order. Gives you time to educate the family what you will be going through.

I did discuss this with Chet's neurologist if the kids should have the blood test that looks for the hereditary type gene that runs in families. She felt it would not benefit them to know if they carry the gene. It would cause undue stress and worry, and there is nothing that can be done unless they volunteered to be in studies for that specific type of Alzheimer's. I told them about the test and they did not want to know.

2BeCourageous updated their status.
December 10, 2014 – 1:23 p.m.
Chet and I and my son and daughter and her husband and their two-year-old son plus two dogs all drove to Michigan the week of Thanksgiving. It went well on the drive there with Chet; he didn't complain and seemed content knowing we were headed home to visit family. He has been asking a lot about Michigan, he would say "Michigan, Michigan" to let me know he was thinking about it. The visits at my moms and sisters house where we stayed went well. The big gathering of the DeBoer side on Thanksgiving also went well. But, on the drive home about four to five hours away from home, major confusion set in and it has not left.

On the way home back to Tennessee where we have lived eight years now, Chet was convinced we were headed in the wrong direction and became very frustrated and agitated. He didn't understand why my son-in-law was driving the wrong direction. He kept saying the church wasn't this way. He was mad that he wasn't stopping to ask what way to go. He was shocked when we told him we were going back home to Tennessee. It seemed like an extra-long drive with his grumbling. Oh, and we watched *Frozen* at least ten times in the van (laughing). I'm still singing the songs!

Since getting back home from the trip, Chet will stand looking very stressed at night and say, "I don't know what to do!" He was up and down a good twenty times, making the bed each time with the dogs and me still in it. One time he said he is dying, another moment he said he is crazy and doesn't know what to do. He won't eat unless you place food in front of him and tell him to eat; he needs help on how to dress. He won't go to bed unless I go to bed with him. Just such a major change in a couple weeks' time.

Each night he is agitated, I was in high hopes he would not do the "sundown syndrome" but he has started it. I will try melatonin and make it lighter in the house. I'd rather try the simple, easy things first than have the doctors overmedicate him.

I think I have finally hit an acceptance point of my husband's disease and feel less angry over all this. I feel more empathy and understanding now and calm when I react to him. This is a devastating disease that takes your loved one's inner self away, friends away, your happily ever after away and it's just plain cruel.

I learned about sundowning from the support groups I belong to. They are a wealth of information and another great place for information is the Alzheimer's Association. I will put links in the back of the book. Sundowning is not a disease, it's a group of symptoms that seem to happen in the evening hours, at least for Chet it did. Chet's symptoms are he paces, he can't stop himself, and his thinking is off—thinking he is dead and being lost. I thought just let him do his thing, eventually, he will tire and come to bed. Wrong! It wears on us having him pace and act all crazy. We felt sorry for him because we knew he couldn't control himself. But, again, it wears on you watching because I'm not getting sleep and Jake isn't getting sleep, so now we are all sleep deprived.

2BeCourageous updated their status.
December 14, 2014 – 10:57 a.m.
Yesterday, our sweet dog, Maggie, went to Heaven; she was in severe congestive heart failure and we had to make that hard decision. This was Chet's love of his life. He spoiled her all the time. I've only seen my husband cry twice but this brought tears and stress to him.

When we got Maggie on Christmas Eve twelve years earlier, Chet was acting like she was no big deal and didn't want to take part in caring for her. If I only could have gotten photos of him holding an umbrella when she went outside to potty when it was raining, or, when the snow was deep, he would shovel paths for her. She would never have to walk to bed, he would carry her to bed with him. She was his dog and he loved her.

2BeCourageous updated their status.
December 16, 2014 – 2:07 a.m.
Chet and I have been married twenty-three years this past July. In that time, I had only seen him cry two times and that was in the late '90s and again when his dad passed away. Since our beloved Maggie, our twelve-year-old shih tzu, passed this past Saturday on 12/13/14, I've watched him cry three times so far over her; his heart is breaking. After weeks on end of extreme confusion has come some sudden clarity in his thinking and reasoning.

Yesterday, Sunday, he told me it was the right thing to do—putting her to sleep—and he even gave me a list of reasons why the decision was best for Maggie, trying to comfort me in the decision I made. This is coming from a man who struggles to communicate and comprehend for his language skills are so affected by the frontotemporal dementia and early-onset Alzheimer's. He has done very well since Saturday. I know it won't last long, but maybe God knew I needed to hear it from my husband. I needed to know he felt right about it even though it has made us feel so bad. Yesterday, we held each other as we both cried. Loss through the death of our pet became a gain to our relationship that's been missed very much. I've learned not to get my hopes up with sudden spells of clarity, but he was there for me, and I could be there to comfort him with good communication on both sides. I'll take it, God's timing always.

I, for the most part, know what my husband is saying though his words can come out in a different order or not at all at times, he gets it across to me. I will also play twenty questions to find out what he is saying if he is having trouble. Sometimes, his words just come out clear as day.

"Love is patient, love is kind. It does not envy, it does not boast, it is not proud. It is not rude, it is not self-seeking, it is not easily angered, it keeps no record of wrongs. Love does not delight in evil but rejoices with the truth. It always protects, always trusts, always hopes, always perseveres."

1 Corinthians 13:4–7 NIV

CHAPTER 15

Be Their Voice

One thing I have learned is you must be your loved one's voice; you should research their medications and read about side effects. Everyone reacts differently to medications, and our personal experience is some medications create more problems than help. This is a disease process that the doctors do not know what causes it and why some patients react one way and another the opposite way. You must take notes in with you to doctor visits, so you can remember what has happened. Don't be afraid to express your concerns because the doctors won't know unless you tell them.

2BeCourageous updated their status.

December 16, 2014 – 9:58 p.m.

Chet had his six-month exam with his neurologist today. She is setting us up with a social worker at Vanderbilt Medical Center to discuss options available for help in the home down the road and options for long-term care if or when needed. I wrote out everything I wanted her to know about the rapid decline in the last few months. I didn't want to list everything verbally in front of Chet and make him upset. The doctor did her in room neuro testing, asking him to repeat a lot of hand motions and have him follow instructions, etc.

I asked where she felt he was at in the disease process. She said, because all the testing she does at appointments is all language-based and his language skills and comprehension is affected, she can't be accurate because of his lack of understanding of words. She said she grades her dementia patients as mild, moderate, late. She said Chet is moderate. She saw a change from the last visit.

She is keeping him on Namenda 10 mg twice a day and Aricept 20 mg a day, and she is adding an antidepressant, Effexor, and will gradually increase it over the next few weeks up to 75 mg a day. I am not a fan of this group of drugs and refused it for him last time. I am on a similar antidepressant in this group and have been overmedicated in the past. I have had adverse effects to psychiatric medications, so that I will be watching him closely. I told her I don't want him overmedicated. It was a good appointment.

2BeCourageous updated their status.

December 17, 2014 – 10:31 p.m.

As most of you know, last June, my son, Jake, got a six-week-old puppy, half lab and half rat terrier; he is all white and about thirty-seven pounds, still growing. His name is Jon Snow; we call him Snow. He has been a bit much for Chet's liking in that Snow is very hyper and naughty as all puppies are. Chet only had the heart for Maggie (our twelve-year-old shih tzu that we put to sleep last Saturday). He didn't like Snow when Snow would pick on Maggie and get too rough.

Snow tore Maggie's eye, playing with her too rough, and she had to have surgery to have it removed in November. I've been keeping an eye on my husband's mood since Mags' passing and he is doing a lot better now, better than I anticipated. I've noticed him petting Snow more and even scratching the dog's belly and talking to him. He didn't give him too much attention before. The dog will lay on him on the couch now too. So, this afternoon, Chet is petting Snow and he says to him, "Well, I guess I like you now."

Me laughing, I yelled loud for my son, Jake, and he hurried out of the den and asked, "What's wrong?"

I said, "Dad had a breakthrough! He just told Snow he likes him now!" Chet started laughing as we all did! It's little things that make us happy and that we celebrate.

2BeCourageous updated their status.
December 31, 2014 – 8:23 p.m.
We have been through a lot this past year—good, bad, happy, and sad—and God has taken care of us wonderfully. He has provided for us every moment. I have made amazing friends around the world this past year on Facebook—in Indonesia, Germany, Australia, Canada, Great Britain just to name a few. How blessed we are to have support groups and friends to make on Facebook. To all my friends and future friends and family, Happy New Year!

2BeCourageous updated their status.
January 04, 2015 – 11:19 p.m.
Chet has been on his new antidepressant for a couple weeks now. He is on the lowest dose (generic Effexor). He is hung over until mid-afternoon, meaning tired and sleeps a lot and, in the evening, he is cheerful and more alive. But he sleeps all night. I give it at night. No wandering the house at night since he has been on it. I have noticed a very noticeable

tremor in his right hand when he holds a drink or silverware. I thought I noticed an ever so mild tremor months ago, but was seldom seen; this increase, I'm sure, is from the antidepressant. He is less grumpy, but the key to that is I am more understanding and accepting.

2BeCourageous updated their status.
January 07, 2015 – 4:24 p.m.

I've been told in the past that you should not pray for patience because it will bring more suffering. I always pray for patience, help, and forgiveness for not having it and becoming an unpleasant person at times. I just don't believe that God is going to hand out tribulations just because I request help dealing with what is on my plate. I believe that the trials and suffering and illnesses are a result of the sinful world we live in and by choices we make for ourselves.

My relationship with God is an up and down one. I'm working on my relationship to be more consistent and loyal with Him as He is with me. I get angry about life, I'm prone to depression at times as I lose my patience with the Alzheimer's disease process and with my body for being in pain from fibromyalgia; I don't always feel good about myself.

By praying for patience, God does deliver when we are ready to receive what He has to give. He has given me calm, at least with my husband's disease, and acceptance. This did not happen overnight, and I kept praying; I had to open myself up to God. Now, that doesn't mean I never get mad or frustrated. It means He is holding my hand and reminds me how to cope, and life is so much better because of that!

Romans 5:1-5 KJV

"Therefore being justified by faith, we have peace with God through our Lord Jesus Christ: by whom also we have access by faith into this grace wherein we stand, and rejoice in hope of the glory of God. And not only so, but we glory in tribulations also: knowing that tribulation worketh patience; and patience, experience; and experience, hope: and hope maketh not ashamed; because the love

of God is shed abroad in our hearts by the Holy Ghost which is given unto us."

2BeCourageous updated their status.
January 09, 2015 – 1:04 a.m.
Very frustrated, Chet ran out of his Aricept two days ago and I called it into the pharmacy for refill the day before he ran out. The pharmacy always calls with an automated message saying it's ready. No call but I had to shop yesterday, so I just went to get it. They can't fill it because insurance won't pay for the two pills a day. I told them they've paid for two pills a day for the last year! Pharmacy faxed the doctor about it. When he was put on Aricept, two pills a day (20 mg), a year ago, the doctor had to call insurance and get permission for one year. The year is up! Ugh! The pharmacy should have called me, so I could contact the doctor right away. Vanderbilt has a patient portal web page plus I could have called. So, I wrote the doctor yesterday; it says the office read it but no response yet. I wrote again today and called and left a message. I will ask pharmacy tomorrow if he can get a day or two to hold him over until this gets settled. What the heck, they know his diagnosis. Why does insurance mess with people like this? He is in a good spell, and I'm nervous him being off the pill this long! Makes me worry! I need to mark the calendar, so I know next year when the year is up, so we don't go through this again.

2BeCourageous updated their status.
January 09, 2015 – 2:34 p.m.
Just talked to the doctor; she just received the paperwork to approve the 20 mg a day and faxed it to the pharmacy, so we should be set! I really like Chet's doctor; she called me once while on maternity leave when I had a question.

2BeCourageous updated their status.
January 30, 2015 – 6:57 p.m.
I love my husband dearly but I sure hate early-onset Alzheimer's and

frontotemporal dementia. It's a love-hate relationship; I love him but hate his diseases ... LOVE WINS!

2BeCourageous updated their status.
February 18, 2015 – 12:30 a.m.
Three weeks completed on the higher dose of the generic Effexor (venla-faxine 75 mg) antidepressant. I have seen a change for the better. Not in memory or cognitive but in his personality. He laughs more and he tries to converse more even though his communication skills are diminished; it's a twenty-question game trying to figure out what he is trying to say sometimes. Though none of the medications (Namenda 20 mg, Aricept 20 mg) seem to have had amazing results, we do not know that for sure, and we do not know where he would be today if he were not on them and could be far worse. This is something we will never know. At least I can see little changes with the antidepressant, and I cherish and welcome those.

2BeCourageous updated their status.
February 28, 2015 – 8:32 p.m.
Chet has had a good week. It's weird, though, in the late fall, he was so cold all the time and sat in the house with a winter coat and gloves on a few times. I know that, with this disease, they get colder than normal. But we just went through our coldest weather yet with ice storms and all and, though most of it melted, he is walking around out back with the dogs with just a pullover sweatshirt. I keep asking him if he is cold and he says no. Go figure. Did I say dogs? Yes, we got a puppy half golden retriever and half husky named Robb Stark. He is three months old now. Chet is truly enjoying the dogs. He tells them both how much he loves them and talks to them without a lot of verbal problems. Dogs are amazing therapy and I'm so glad we got them. I thought to lose his Maggie, our twelve-year-old shih tzu, this past December was going to advance him in his disease, but he has handled it well.

The highlight of Chet's month, though, is going to the local Chinese buffet restaurant in La Vergne and eating the mystery stuff they put in the shells. (Laughing) We fill a whole plate with just that for him, then he piles another plate with all the other stuff. If they happen not to have those, he will pout the rest of the day. No matter when I ask him what he wants to eat, he says "Chinese!" with a childlike grin hoping I will say yes. (Laughing) I can't say there has been a decline in the last month or two, he is about the same but laughs more since putting him on the antidepressant. Having a loved one with dementia is hard for the whole family, having a spouse with early-onset changes everything. (End post.)

****

This reminded me of the time in 2013, my husband just got a new hat and he thought he looked great in it and he did. Well, what else? Yep, he lost it. I gave up looking; we searched everywhere. I said, "You are on your own. I do not know where else to look!" So, he thought a moment, and he said maybe he took it off at the Chinese restaurant we were at earlier in the day and walked out without it. He was still okay to drive when this happened, and I didn't want to go with him. So, he went there and asked if they found a hat. A man brought out two hats.

The man asked, "Are one of these yours?"

Chet came home; I said, "Did you find your hat?"

"YES, TWO!" he said laughing hard! They were both his; he had left the other one there another time who knows when. Hahaha.

The guy said to him, "We'll make you a box with your name on it." Hahaha, I died laughing! No idea when he left the other one there. Thank goodness, we can laugh.

2BeCourageous updated their status.
March 17, 2015 – 1:43 a.m.

Sometimes humor, no matter how strange, gets us through. I'm starting to think the key to not having bad days and to prevent regression in these dementia diseases is never to announce that your loved one has good days.

Never brag that there has been no regressing or decline for some time. Because, sure enough, as soon as you let those happy words out beyond your lips, your words magically turn into little destructive, skull-penetrating, brain-cell-killing death rays. Alarms go off in your loved one's head yelling, "Danger! Danger! Positive words have entered the atmosphere! Shut down! Prepare for decline!" Then, no sooner had you said those nice things, your words betray you and make a liar out of you. In turn, it makes you look delusional, like you have no idea really what the heck is going on with your loved one! They take ten steps backward and end up in new territory we have not explored. A state that couldn't be further from the one you claimed a week ago, so now you know why and how decline happens in dementia patients—it's caregivers bragging on those good days! So, yeah, just thought you should know the truth. True story last week sucked.

– Heidi

2BeCourageous updated their status.
March 20, 2015 – 4:44 p.m.
I was answering some research interview questions the other day about my husband and his dementia (EOA and FTD). The last question asked was, "What do I miss about him pre-diagnosis?" I wanted to say EVERYTHING and leave it at that. There was so much to say, and I knew they did not want to know every single detail. There was only a small line to write so much on.

Like, when he used to look at me, I could see into his sparkly eyes and see into his soul how much he loves me. Those glimpses are not so often now, not because he loves me less, but because I can no longer read his expressions; many times his eyes seem empty.

Another is that half-grin he would get on his face trying to cover up his disappointment or anger at losing a game. His inability to tell a joke, laughing through the entire thing then forgetting the punch line. Him being able to read my mind and know what my needs were. I miss the security his hugs made me feel. I miss his leadership. I miss his encouragement through God's word. I miss our two-way conversations on why God does what He does. Or just reminiscing the old days. I miss his teasing me and making me laugh. I missed his positive outlook when life ganged up on us. I miss dreaming together how life would be when we retire. I miss making up after an argument. (Blushing). I also miss his cooking; he was the most amazing cook.

There is no way you can sum it up in one sentence; he is and was much more than a sentence. He was and still is my world. That world has changed, missing these things is all part of the daily grief process—grieving the pieces that turn up missing, grieving him while he is still alive.

His love for me is not missing, and my love for him will always be, in this world and the next. That will never change, that is not part of the pieces missing in action.

– 2BeCourageous, where love wins.

"Let no corrupting talk come out of your mouths, but only such as is good for building up, as fits the occasion, that it may give grace to those who hear."

EPHESIANS 4:29 ESV

CHAPTER 16

THE STRAW THAT BROKE THE CAMEL'S BACK

Every time you can find humor in a difficult situation, *love wins.*

2BeCourageous updated their status.
April 11, 2015 – 10:15 p.m.

My tongue can cut like a knife when I become overwhelmed and impatient, then the guilt from that is like a whip upon myself; not a good coping day. This just gets harder. A lot of pain today.

2BeCourageous was feeling drained.
April 22, 2015 – 3:29 p.m.

We have entered down a new road on this journey we are on. It's a bumpy one too. Chet is forgetting how to do proper hygiene now and needs me to guide him in his daily routine. I have taken over his shaving for him too. Yesterday, the concept of washing his hands was foreign to him; I had to walk him through it. This comes and goes. Also, putting on and taking off clothes now can get very confusing for him. Some days he just can't figure it out and gets very overwhelmed by it. He can't be left alone anymore. Please pray for our family as we venture down this one way, dead end road.

2BeCourageous updated their status.
April 27, 2015 – 8:27 a.m.
My daughter's father-in-law died suddenly of a massive heart attack at age fifty-five on April 23rd, 2015. We went to his funeral and Chet did well there; it was filled with loving bikers giving great testimony about Mike, Brandon's dad.

A very sad time for our families.

2BeCourageous updated their status.
May 03, 2015 – 10:19
Chet has been said to have FTD and early-onset Alzheimer's. He was described of his language difficulties as logopenic primary progressive aphasia, but, reading about it, he fits the agrammatic type and the semantic type that explain him better. I think it's all a guessing game.

2BeCourageous updated their status.
May 07, 2015 – 9:34 p.m.
Next week, I need to get a power of attorney papers and the will, I should have done it two years ago but didn't. Chet's twenty-four-month waiting period is up in June for him being able to go on Medicare through Social Security Disability. I just signed him up for Humana Medicare Advantage plan that has prescription coverage and then tried to cancel the plan Medicare automatically put him on.

Well, of course, they wanted Chet to verify his birthdate, address, name, and give them permission to talk to me! That did not go well;

I had his birthdate typed out in large numbers so he could read it. He couldn't. He couldn't tell them his last name even. He got "Chet" out but not "Chester." So, the guy with a strong accent and hard to understand said he would say the information to him, and all he has to say is yes or no if it's correct. The best he could do was say okay. He just couldn't get the answers out. Finally, he said yes, they could talk with me! I knew I had to get a power of attorney and, thank God, I have someone that will help, but don't put it off like I did, get it done! I'm getting power of attorney over health and financial and the will.

2BeCourageous updated their status.
May 19, 2015 – 1:24 a.m.
I was reminding Chet to take his night pills that I had put out for him. He looked at them and, for the first time in three to four years, asked me what they are for. I went down the list showing him each one, explaining this one is for blood pressure, this one for cholesterol, these two are for diabetes, and these two are for Alzheimer's. He says, "Oh that's me!" laughing ....

Then he asked what the last one was for and I told him, "That one, when you take it, makes you think I seem like a really hot, sexy momma!" He burst out laughing! (Me laughing.)

I teased him and said, "Hey! That wasn't the right time to burst out laughing!"

He said, "Oh, I don't need pills for that, I think that already!"

Aww, so sweet! Even with dementia, he still knows how to cover his butt! Hahaha, I cherish the moments his humor breaks through!

2BeCourageous updated their status.
June 05, 2015 – 12:59 a.m.
Well, Chet went to bed mad at me and not speaking to me because I insisted that he should get out of his dirty clothes and put on his pajamas to go to bed tonight. He insisted he does not change out of his clothes to go to bed and I argued with him. (I know, I know—don't argue with

dementia patients because they believe they are right and you cannot win! Hmm, I might have dementia also then!) So, anyways, I argued with him over it when explaining it sensibly got me nowhere. I let him keep his T-shirt on from the day, just got him to change his pants to jammie pants and take his shoes off. Tomorrow, I will have to insist he take a shower, and hoping he welcomes this idea because he has seemed to stop doing so on his own. I have had him cat bath himself (washing with a washcloth over the sink) and remind him to brush his teeth. This is so not him; Mr. Clean himself showered daily and never wore the same outfit two days in a row. It's like I'm learning how to raise a child all over again, this time around, though, it happens to be my husband and he can't learn because he forgets.

2BeCourageous commented on their post.
June 06, 2015 – 7:47 p.m.
My friend told me an idea for husbands or wives—done with her husband to save arguments, etc.—she showered with him since she needed to anyway. I thought that really is a good idea and hadn't considered doing that, I may see how that goes!

Update: It went well. I can see a problem when he no longer knows me, though; then we will get a shower chair and sprayer.

2BeCourageous updated their status.
June 18, 2015 – 3:32 a.m.
Sometimes, 2-Be-Courageous means being there for your loved one as their world changes forever, and reassuring them they are not alone in the battles they face.

2BeCourageous updated their status.
June 25, 2015 – 9:30 p.m.
Love is contagious. Fear is contagious. Dementia is not contagious but spreads fear. To counteract that fear, help spread the love.

2BeCourageous updated their status.
June 28, 2015 – 3:34 p.m.
"Living with a Parent with Dementia While a Teenager … Our House."

2BeCourageous are our twins, Jake and Chessie, soon to be twenty-one on July 19th, 2015, and my son-in-law, Brandon (22). They are a blessing, and I'm so proud of them. It's not easy at all having your father develop early-onset Alzheimer's/FTD while you are in high school and not know what is wrong or why his personality and abilities are changing before your eyes.

Imagine what it must feel like as a teenager being told your dad has dementia and that there is no cure. No treatment to hold it off, no remissions, only medications to alleviate some symptoms for a year or two at most. Then the medication stops working, and nothing slows the progression of the disease at all.

It is heartbreaking and scary watching your dad slowly change. Unable to remember most of his past and having the present-day happenings only stay in memory maybe a day or so. Admiring him as your hero growing up, the leader of the family, a college degree and business owner, and very independent. Then suddenly turning completely dependent and unable to work or communicate well in just a couple short years.

Our kids are handling this well, though I'm not sure what lies deep within. Chessie comes over and spends the day with us bringing our grandson, Braydon, age three, with her four to five days a week. Braydon loves his Grandpa Chet and, at three, is aware grandpa needs help at times and runs to help him when he can! Brandon, our son-in-law, visits here at our house after work often, and, many days, we all share dinner as a family around the table.

My son, Jake, lives with us while he is in college and is so wonderful with his dad and they are all very patient and kind with him. Jake is a great help to me and helps keep my sanity in check by making me laugh and engages me in our long midnight talks. I couldn't be prouder of them all; it has not been an easy adjustment or life for things change quickly with this disease, and grieving each new piece that is lost is part of it. But what's great about my twins and son-in-law is they all know and understand the meaning of family commitment, love, and God!

Young people today are having to be caregivers in their homes because dementia is growing in large numbers. I like to think of it as family loving on family; I think that's how God wants us to see it. Though I know it's not always possible in every home, we are very blessed to have each other. Love wins.

2BeCourageous updated their status.
July 11, 2015 – 11:22 p.m.

We adventured out today; Jake and Chet and I went to the movies—*Jurassic World*! The *Jurassic Park* series was always a favorite of ours. I have not been to a movie since 2010. I was so excited to get out once we left the house! We were not sure if we should bring Chet and was hoping someone could watch him, but it didn't work out. He complains a lot at home about what's on the TV and falls asleep during everything and panics when he has to go to the bathroom suddenly sometimes. My biggest fear was he can no longer tolerate loud noises. He plugs his ears if we get too loud at home. So, we stopped on the way and bought him ear plugs! All that worry I did and he sat there the whole time, focused; we held hands, and I tried to shake his hand if I could tell something scary or startling was about to happen, so he would not get startled bad. He didn't need the earplugs! He did great! That made me so happy! It felt so good to get out and do something fun! We hardly ever go anywhere nowadays except to a grocery store.

During this timeframe, things started to get worse quickly. Chet goes into panic mode when he has to go to the bathroom; he no longer is sure where the bathrooms are, and it seems he waits until his bladder is about to burst. At least, that's the impression he gives. I have put signs and arrows in the hallway and on the bathroom doors, so he knows which rooms are the bathroom. I also put signs on our bedrooms, listing it as "Chet's Bedroom," "Jake's Den," "Jake's Bedroom." He is starting to have bowel issues also, more diarrhea and has trouble making it to the bathroom sometimes. We now carry emergency clothes to change into in the car should he have an accident. Watching your better half fading away creates, early on, a void, and an ever-changing realm of grief.

– Heidi

2BeCourageous updated their status.
August 06, 2015 – 11:32 p.m.
Because my husband's speech and cognition was one of the first things to be affected, I do not always know what he is trying to say or tell me. Or, he will say something that makes complete sense sentence-wise, but it isn't really what he meant or wanted to say or on the topic.

Now, I am very aware what is to come down the road as far as who he may remember or who he may not remember. I think we all fear not being remembered! I also think we or, at least, I tuck that thought away in the back of my mind because it's a scary thing to keep fretting over and worrying about it. So, I try to block what may come and just deal with today, the here and now! Yesterday to Chet is gone, we can't talk about it or reminisce; he doesn't remember it most days.

As we were sitting watching TV tonight, Chet looked at me and said, "Do you stay here all the time?"

It threw me off and I just stared at him a second or two. I said, "What do you mean? Like do I live here all the time?"

He responded, "Yes."

I said, "I live here with you all the time."

He said, "Okay, good!"

I asked, "Is that what you wanted to know?"

He said, "Yeah, that's good!"

I'm still not sure if that's what he meant. But I didn't let it get me all emotional. Well, maybe a little! I told my son, Jake, what he said and Jake told me that, when I go out shopping without Chet and leave him with Jake, Chet searches for me constantly and isn't happy and asks for me.

When I walk in the door, he runs to me and hugs me and says, "There you are, I'm so happy to see you!" I was only gone thirty minutes, but I will take that any day over him not seeming to care or not knowing who I am. Have a good night or day depending what side of the world you are on and God bless. Hugs.

– Heidi DeBoer at 2BeCourageous on Facebook.

2BeCourageous was feeling amused.
August 16, 2015 – 2:32 p.m.
In my mind, everything said can be made into a musical, which means I can come up with a song to about anything said in this house! Which really means I sing a lot and off key! I was singing in the kitchen "I Will Always Love You" more in a screechy opera style to Chet. He turned around, stood on his tiptoes, and put his hands together and started doing his own opera style singing, "I LOVE YOU, YOU, YOU, YOU" until he got real high key and couldn't anymore. I love when his sense of humor breaks through and he gets silly!

2BeCourageous updated their status.
August 20, 2015 12:30 a.m.
Well, it was a crappy day, literally. Chet has been having bowel incontinence because he has chronic diarrhea on and off for several months now, more on than off lately, a big reason we don't travel far from home! I was suspecting his Alzheimer's medication, Aricept, because that is a side effect. But he is seeing a GI specialist for it now and he is running tests, trying to rule things out. It might be his diabetes meds, metformin, he said. I hope it turns out that simple to resolve!

He had a diarrhea accident in the grocery store last week while with Jake, my twenty-one-year-old son. Jake called me to ask me to bring clothes to Kroger. When I got there to the men's room, Jake had Chet's clothes off; all the clothes were messed on the inside, and he had him all cleaned up in the handicap stall. I was so proud of my son for taking care of his dad like that because he gags and leaves the room when we changed my grandson's diapers! Chet's had accidents before, so we bought adult diapers but they seem to leak out. We only had him wear them when we go out. But after another BM blowout at home today and his second shower, he is in them until we can fix the problem, if we can fix the problem.

I know this is really on the personal side and I debated to write about it. But it's part of our journey with this disease, and I know others deal with this same thing. Maybe something I say will help someone else, if nothing else make them feel less alone in this horrible disease, having someone else to relate to!

He has to see a surgeon on August 31st about a tumor I discovered on his thigh a few weeks back. To me, it feels like a fatty tumor, at least that's what I want it to be! But can a man that has no fat left in his body have a fatty tumor? Don't know! He is very thin and looks much older than his years now. In fact, the last three doctors in the last few weeks asked how I was related to him. Um yeah! His wife of twenty-four years related! I told Chet it must be my new strawberry blonde hair, makes me look younger! (Laughing)

So, what else did today bring? Oh, I asked Chet to let the dog that was jumping at the back door in. Then I heard Chet having a panic attack session, trying to tell us something but couldn't get it out. I looked up and there is my lovely dog, Robb, covered in wet (just rained), fresh mud (like mud wrestling muddy) all over his feet and legs and all over his belly, and dark, muddy footprints all over my carpet and floors. The mud was dripping off him, then he lay down!

Jake cleaned up the house, carpets still stained! I washed both dogs with the hose outside, since Mr. Muddy had jumped on me, I was now covered in mud too! Grrrrr. This was after Chet's two blowout ordeals in the morning! The muddy dog, Robb, was freaking out on the leash and tried to take off with my finger wrapped in the leash; I think it may be fractured, I could hear it crack when he took off. I was muddy, soaked with water and sweat afterward, and I took a cold drink and got in the shower and just stood there for a long time. No, I don't usually drink and shower at the same time, it was just needed today! Hugs.

– Heidi DeBoer

Update: The tumor was a fatty tumor, and the surgeon said, considering Chet's Alzheimer's and where he is at with it, he would just leave the tumor alone and watch it. Sigh.

2BeCourageous updated their status.
August 21, 2015 – 1:03 a.m.
A skunk was the straw that broke the camel's back! Robb got skunked! A gallon of tomato juice and Dawn dish soap and I'm soaked and smelly again after midnight. I love my dog, really; but, today, he wasn't high on my list. (Laughing so I don't cry.)

2BeCourageous updated their status.
August 23, 2015 – 12:19 a.m.
The gastro doctor called and said Chet's blood tests and stool tests are normal. So, the next move is to stop his diabetes medication, metformin 1000 mg at two times a day, for two weeks because that causes diarrhea. We stopped it yesterday. His primary care physician nurse called yesterday about it also because the gastro doc called their office. It concerned me that they weren't substituting another med for the metformin. The nurse said, "Oh, he will be fine."

I said, "If he will be fine without it, then he really doesn't need it in the first place!" Time will tell, he is still on the glimepiride for it.

2BeCourageous updated their status.
September 03, 2015 – 9:55 p.m.
It's been a long two weeks. Two weeks ago, we took away Chet's metformin, 2000 mg a day, for his diabetes per the request of his gastrointestinal specialist. He wanted him off it, after testing came back normal, to see

why he is having liquid diarrhea more on than off the last six months. He went downhill so badly these last two weeks, I can only blame it on diabetes levels being off. His counts yesterday at the doctors was around 450. Tonight it's 436. Was lower in the 200s during the day. He has had no sweets at all. He is not able to find the bathroom in the house on his own, he panics and groans like he must pee now and no stopping it! We have signs up leading to the bathroom. They do not help at all anymore.

Well, with his counts so high, he is spilling sugar in his urine and peeing more, and it's urgent! His confusion doubled and his neediness on me tripled. It doesn't sound nice but that wears on you a lot, being followed every step you make and being told "I love you" every sixty seconds! Listening to "I don't know what to do" over and over. When I ask him to do anything at all, he has no idea what I'm talking about for the most part. I asked him to close the curtains in the living room tonight, and he went to the refrigerator and said he doesn't know where they are. I asked him this week to take off his shoes to get ready for bed and he takes one off and then the other, and puts the other right back on if I don't sit next to him and guide him. He gets mad because I insist his shoes must come off to get his pants off and he tells me that's nonsense!

I got a new glucose meter yesterday; I do not think the one I had been using on him was reading his levels right! They were nowhere near what he read yesterday at the doctor's office. The new meter is reading higher levels. I had no idea his levels were so high. I am not happy that the doctors did not put him on something else right away. I am not happy with myself that I didn't stand up and say do it! You know, you hold on to that hope that a doctor may know what they are doing. But if your gut says, "No, this isn't right," then we need to act on it. If we do not stand up for our loved ones, no one else will! What he lost these last two weeks in functioning, I do not believe he will get back when his sugar levels come down. I think the damage is done.

Update: They have him on a new medication now. Injections but not insulin.

There are some theories out there among the 100s of what causes early-onset Alzheimer's. Some call it diabetes of the brain and they believe that the blood sugar levels, somehow, are killing the brain cells. Do not know enough about it even to explain it. But, watching my husband, I'm starting to believe that. There are also articles written that metformin can cause dementia. I hope that is fake news.

Oh, the diarrhea did stop, but now is loose to normal. He did have an accident the other day at a Chinese restaurant in the men's room only because someone was in the only stall and I was standing outside waiting for him. I heard his groans starting and then banging (he was banging on the stall door), and then a strange voice yelling, "Use the woman's bathroom!" Oh my gosh! I went in there but it was too late; luckily, I had clean clothes in the car for him. The Depend diaper leaked. I had no idea someone was in there with him. It's hard to want to take him places; I feel so sorry for him because he cannot help any of this! On the up side of all this, I've been very calm with him; I think it's finally sunk in my heart and head that this is our life. Thanks for reading this. Hugs to you all in this type of journey!

2BeCourageous updated their status.
September 04, 2015 – 9:47 p.m.
Chet is on the generic form of Effexor and has done him well, but I think it's time to increase it. I said no to increasing it a year ago, I don't want him zombied out and he sleeps a lot now anyway. I told them I would know when it's time to increase and now it's time, I think.

2BeCourageous updated their status.
September 07, 2015 – 10:50 p.m.
Chet's sisters, Joyce and Susan, came to visit from Michigan this weekend. Chet has trouble coming up with words and understanding them at times, but, singing gospel songs, he nails and does well. He sat on the couch with his two sisters and they sang gospel songs acapella, and the words flowed out his mouth beautifully. They sounded like angels. Chet's

other sister, Peg, is fighting her own battles with cancer and is unable to travel. We love and miss her.

2BeCourageous updated their status.
September 22, 2015 – 12:29 a.m.

Lights out, sitting on the couch cuddled up next to my husband, him rubbing my shoulders while we watch a movie together. Everything feels well and normal, caught up in the moment as if this disease never existed, slipping into the comfort of lost familiarity. And though the movie is long over, I've captured those two hours in my heart, not wanting to let them go.

*"And when you stand praying, if you hold anything against anyone,
forgive them, so that your Father in heaven may forgive you your
sins."*

MARK 11:25 NIV

CHAPTER 17

THE PEOPLE IN THE MIRROR

2BeCourageous updated their status.
October 04, 2015 – 6:02 p.m.

Well, everyone has a Walmart story. Here is mine. Chet and I went shopping the other day for warm shirts for him and a pair of jeans for me. As I was assigned a dressing room so I could try on pants, I told the lady that Chet would be coming in with me. She got very huffy and a stern face and told me, "No, he cannot go in there with you!"

I said, number one, he is my husband and, number 2, he has early-onset Alzheimer's. "I will leave him out here with you and you can watch him and be responsible for him then!"

She looked disgusted and huffed out a breath and said, "Fine! You can use that room instead!" (Handicap one.) I so wanted to make groaning noises and bang on the wall when we were in there together and make it sound like mad, passionate love! Should have! Laughing!

2BeCourageous updated their status.
October 11, 2015 – 1:20 a.m.
After getting Chet ready for bed last night and got him all tucked in, this limited conversation took place:

> Chet: "You!"
> Heidi: "Me? What about me?"
> Chet: "I don't know!"
> Heidi: "What don't you know?"
> Chet: "You!"
> Heidi: "You don't know me? Do you know my name?"
> Chet: (after a long confused pause) "I don't know. No, sorry."
> Heidi: "It's Heidi. Do you know who I am to you?"
> Chet: (long pause) "No."
> Heidi: "I'm your wife; we are married; you are the love of my life."
> Chet: "Really?! Wow! Really?!"

Sometimes I would like to just wake up from this nightmare and have him grin and point at me and say, "Gotcha!"

He tells me he loves me every five minutes, which makes me feel guilty in a way because I take it as a sign of him being insecure that I don't love him back; I respond right back at him that I love him too. He says it even more often if I am short-tempered that day. So, I know it is insecurity. He says to me, "You are such a kind person, thank you for doing this! You are wonderful!" after I help him in the bathroom after he goes.

More guilt because I'm thinking in my head, *No, I'm not wonderful. I hate helping you in some of these very private ways!* But I will do it because I love him and committed my life to him. He follows me every step I make in the house, some days I insist he sit and just wait for me to come back into the room instead of following me. That doesn't always work, and he is right behind. The two dogs are not any better, so I have three following me to the bathroom! Me and my shadows! I told him yesterday we are in this together for the long haul and that I would be right by his side always.

I do believe, as his neurologist said this week, that his language skills have worsened and the words do not always make sense to him, and he cannot speak a complete sentence and have it make sense anymore. There are no more two-way conversations and I miss that! So, not knowing my name or how to describe who I am to him isn't that he doesn't know the answers, it is his brain won't always let him make sense of the words he hears or wants to say. But he has told me more than once now he doesn't know me.

My son and daughter and son-in-law were away for a week last week in Iowa, and I asked Chet if he missed Jake (he lives with us and has never been gone this long since the dementia began), Chet said, "Who?"

I said, "Jakie, your son."

He said he didn't know who that was. Later, he saw a picture of Jake on my computer and immediately said, "Hey, there's Jake!" all excited to see his face. I really want to believe he knows us 100% because, when he see's people in the store he knows, he gets all excited and happy but can't come up with their name. His language and learning skills were hit the hardest and continue to get worse, and memory is bad, no doubt; but, when your brain betrays you and what you know and what you say become two different things, it's hard to know where he really stands as far as stages and progression.

I need to add here that him not knowing me hurt, but I knew this day was coming and I was prepared. What I wasn't prepared for was, while going through my daughter's wedding photos, Chet didn't know who she was and didn't recognize himself in them either. This hit me harder and I've never had the heart to tell my daughter this. Chet was so proud that he remembered the wedding a month later but, now, at over a year later, he doesn't even recognize himself or his daughter, and it still brings tears writing this.

On a brighter note, Chessie brought back photos on her phone of their trip to Brandon's grandma in Iowa. As I was scrolling through them, up came a photo of a pregnancy test kit that said pregnant on it. My mouth fell open, and I started saying, "Really? Really?" I was so excited for them. Due in June 2016. They had been trying!

2BeCourageous updated their status.
October 16, 2015 – 10:37 p.m.
I filled out a questionnaire for a trial of medication for dementia for Chet, then read more on it. After reading more on it, I saw which is standard with all trials that they will use a placebo (sugar pill, fake). So, you won't know if the real drug is being administered. I guess, what is stopping me from moving forward should they call us to be a part is, after the trial is over twenty-six weeks or so, you won't be able to take the real medication anymore. So, if you did get the real drug and it somehow improved you in the areas it said it might and life gets some better, bam—the trial is over and you have no choice. You can't take the drug that showed improvement anymore. So, we would see a better change by chance and then watch him go back to as he was? How is that even fair? There are a lot of "ifs" and "mights" in this, but, if I saw my husband improve and have it taken away and the drug won't be approved for five to seven years, well, I don't know; great for others down the road, I know it is! But it's already messed with my emotions of just thinking of this happening to my husband. I'm not sure what I'm supposed to be feeling or if this is wrong to feel. I would be crushed and heartbroken if I saw my old husband come back and leave again! (Chet didn't qualify after all, he is too far advanced. I stressed for nothing.)

2BeCourageous updated their status.
December 11, 2015 – 2:18 a.m.
Dear Lord, give me strength! My dog, Robb, who was sound asleep on the bathroom floor, and the bathroom rug and towel I keep around the toilet on the floor all got peed on; Chet didn't even hit the toilet. The worst part besides the dog being peed on was the surprise from my husband when I was asking for him to stop, which, of course, he couldn't!

He says, "What's wrong? Why are you upset?" was the reaction I got.

My response, "Um, you just peed on the dog!" Ugh! Another bath, but not his fault this time! Laughing, poor dog.

2BeCourageous was feeling overwhelmed.
December 19, 2015 – 1:00 a.m.

I haven't posted much on this page lately, I guess because I've been so down and each different doctor appointment for Chet has nothing good to say. It's like, how can one person have so much wrong suddenly? I also like humor and use it wherever I can, and I have run out of humor this week. I've been fighting my own health battle and demons on top of it. I hurt my back, we think, by lifting large landscaping rocks to build border walls for my garden. So, I have a herniated disk that popped on me and now is pressing on the sciatic nerve at the bottom on my spine. I thought I knew pain with my fibromyalgia and past horse riding accidents. But, no, God wanted me to experience something new, sarcastically said. It's nonstop all the way down my leg to my foot that is numb. I think the pain pills make me very emotional because I have not cried this much since my dad died in 2003. Starting physical therapy next week. I know God didn't do this, by the way.

Chet has several new health issues. He has had blood in his urine on and off, and the urologist could not get the scope into the bladder because he has two strictures that have narrowed the urethra, so he must have surgery on January 12th to have it widened. They want him knocked out and the anesthesia part scares me. I've heard stories where it can make dementia worse. Also, the urologist did a CAT scan and it showed a kidney stone and a one-inch mass on one kidney that is solid and 70% chance of cancer. The doctor said he would have to think long and hard on what action to take on that. He is going to see if it's in a position where he can freeze it, but not sure.

Chet had an abnormal EKG, so we went to a heart specialist and he said Chet has an inherited heart disease that can cause sudden death. He has not had an abnormal EKG before, so this made no sense, but he must have an echocardiogram in January, and he said he didn't think Chet could tolerate the other heart testing he'd like to run.

We went to the foot doctor also this week to get medicine for fungus infections on both his feet. We also went to an endocrinologist this week to get control of his diabetes that we lost control of when we removed him from his metformin that was causing severe diarrhea in him. All these appointments in one week have worn both of us out.

Chet didn't know himself a few times this week; he brought me his wallet that we keep his driver's license in it for ID purposes, and he told me that wasn't his wallet because that is not his photo and he doesn't know who that is in there and we should give it back. He doesn't recognize himself in wedding photos at my daughter's wedding this week either. One time at the hospital, he was taking a long time in the men's room, so I peeked in and he was standing in the middle of the floor, staring at himself in the mirror. I asked what he was doing and he said, "Waiting for him," the guy in the mirror; he was referring to himself.

So, I'm feeling overwhelmed right now by all this and trying to manage everything for Christmas and trying to make it a nice one, and worrying about finances this month and all the other normal daily stuff, so, if you pray, please pray for us or send nice thoughts our way ... God bless you all!

2BeCourageous updated their status.
December 25, 2015 – 2:06 p.m.
Anesthesia is a common concern in the dementia world. I belong to several support groups online and it comes up over and over how the patient has negative effects after anesthesia that are lasting; not everyone but it does happen and Chet is not your typical Alzheimer's patient, he has mixed dementia that's very aggressive. Appreciate your prayers for the 12th, he has his surgery then. Merry Christmas everyone and God bless. Hugs

2BeCourageous was feeling emotional.
January 08, 2016 – 10:56 p.m.

Sundowning has begun, and it makes him agitated and mean. He threatened me last night by storming down the hallway behind me because I got out of bed; it was still early and he was breathing fast and hard behind me, and I turned around to see a mad fierce face, as in angry and crazed, coming at me. I yelled for Jake because he scared me and Jake came right out to calm him down. Tonight, he threatened to hit me.

I've learned that, when he says he wants to go home, he doesn't mean his home or an old home—he means his bed. He wants to go to bed, he is tired. But he won't stay in bed, he is up and down and up and down over and over, and his speech no longer makes sense, so he gets mad at me when I don't understand what he is saying to me. Tonight, he wanted to go home before 7:00 p.m. I said fine, I got him undressed and ready for bed, I usually encourage him to stay up longer and watch TV with me, but he wasn't happy doing that either. He did his up and down routine, and, about the tenth time out to the living room, I asked Jake if he would show Chet to his bed; I had just got a bowl of cereal and sat down and I wanted to watch TV. Well, not even five minutes later, he was back up and came walking so fast down the hall with his crazed look on his face. He got to me in the living room and bent over, so his angry face was looking into mine, and I asked, "What are you doing?" He made a fist and drew it back and swung halfway to my face and I screamed for Jake. I spilled my cereal and I started crying. Chet snapped out of his crazed look and was all apologetic saying I'm sorry over and over, staying in my face until I said I was okay. I had to go to bed with him, so he would stay in there. Jake said we need sleep medicine for him. Tonight, I gave him two Benadryl, so he would sleep … I'm so sad right now. My husband would never hit me or threaten me ever. This is a night thing, he isn't like this all day long. It's called sundowning. I hate this disease that has taken my husband's mind away.

2BeCourageous updated their status.
January 10, 2016 – 10:35 p.m.

Dear Lord, please give me patience and wisdom tonight! My husband has told me he is dead at least six times tonight while he is wandering the house and up and down, in and out of bed. He is talking away but most of it I'm not sure what he is saying. Usually, me being in bed with him calms him and he will go to sleep, but, two [doses of] melatonin later, he is wired! Most likely a reaction from the melatonin or Benadryl. I have written his neurologist and told her all the events of the last week and she will get that email in the morning. I told her he needs sleep meds!

2BeCourageous updated their status.
January 12, 2016 – 1:21 p.m.

We are at the hospital and they are going to take Chet back for his procedure any minute now. It's a hurry-up-and-wait kind of morning and afternoon. He has been sleeping.

2BeCourageous updated their status.
January 12, 2016 – 2:43 p.m.

The doctor came in and said everything went good, and said he cut the strictures open and feels the blood we have been seeing has been caused by infection up behind the strictures. The bladder looked good. He said the strictures could come back and we will have to do it again. We talked a little about the mass on the kidney, and it is too far in to freeze it. So, it can be removed but, right now, I think he is opting to watch it. Will know more in a month. He said it is two centimeters and when they are three centimeters and up is when they start to spread, so he wants to watch it, hmmm. He did say he can see where Chet can be a handful! Not sure what that meant; he must have given them a bit of trouble, not sure. Waiting for him to come back to the room. Not sure how long he has to stay after that or if he can go home. He said he wrote Monday on the orders but said, after thinking about it, he decided we can remove the catheter on Friday. Anesthesia Doc just came in and said Chet did well, no trouble at all! They made sure to use non-mind-altering drugs on him.

2BeCourageous updated their status.
January 12, 2016 – 6:41 p.m.
We have been home a good hour and it's going to be a long few days until Friday when we can take the catheter out. His hands go for it and he wants to pull it out and forgets from one conversation about it to the next why it's there and that he has to pee through it. They gave me a syringe to help remove it, and the doc didn't say what time Friday, so, as soon as midnight hits, I'll be like, "Okay, get err done!" (Laughing) Oh, Lord, give me patience! Jake came up with an idea to put an apron on him, so it's harder to get to. Chet didn't like that idea! But he is wearing it anyway.

2BeCourageous updated their status.
January 12, 2016 – 8:44 p.m.
Not sure I can take much more. I have two dogs with such a bad flea dermatitis allergy going, and I can't get control of it because my back pain won't let me bathe them, and we can't be out of the house long enough to treat it properly. They are suffering itching constantly, and I've tried so many treatments already, and they can't stand themselves. Plus, my husband keeps trying to pull his catheter out every five minutes, saying he didn't know it was there and is making no sense whatsoever, and I'm tired of hurting; my body is screaming.

2BeCourageous updated their status.
January 13, 2016 – 2:05 p.m.
I get my break away by going to physical therapy; there is an improvement today, hoping it stays that way. Oh, Vanderbilt Social Services called me today and gave me numbers to get in home help to see if we qualify through the Choices Program. I ask if they had a program where Jake could get paid to be a caregiver and they do, but he isn't allowed to live in the house! Drats!

2BeCourageous was feeling accomplished.
January 15, 2016 – 12:32 a.m.

Well, I was determined today to get things done. Two dogs bathed and deflead, one house vacuumed with furniture moved and cushions removed and vacuumed under, vacuumed along all the baseboards with a hose. Dusted and then took tree down and put Christmas decorations away. Sprayed furniture and carpet for fleas, washed all my bedding, washed the dogs' kennel bedding, and washed all the throw blankets. Made homemade chili and cornbread for dinner and removed my husband's catheter twelve hours early to calm him. Oh, and washed the living room drapes. So, yeah, take that back pain and sciatica, you will not hold me down! (I probably won't be such a smart aleck in the morning!)

2BeCourageous updated their status.
January 15, 2016 – 3:15 a.m.

Yesterday, I felt I failed miserably as a wife, friend, and caregiver. I feel I made my husband cry. I took the catheter that he had in from his surgery out early (the doctor gave his okay) because Chet continuously played with it and pulled on it, trying to pull it out and there was no reasoning with him. He had it after his stricture surgery so the urethra could heal. He had no idea why it was there. I explained and re-explained why he needed it. So did my son. But it was like he never heard us. He was happy it was out until he had to pee, which happened to be right when I had everything off of him, putting on clean clothes and a Depend. He couldn't make it to the toilet and it hurt horribly. Frustrated, I did an "I told you that it would be painful" and I was upset saying it. He broke out crying very hard, which shocked me, and I felt horrible. He kept saying it hurts, it hurts. I apologized and comforted him and calmed him and told him I loved him so much. He kept crying hard saying how much it hurt. I got him in bed and then I got in the shower and just fell apart crying. My husband is forgiving, Alzheimer's is even more forgiving in its own cruel way. Today, I will try harder; it broke my heart to see him fall apart in pain but he was going to do more damage trying to pull the catheter out, so I took it out.

Update: Dogs are on antibiotics and flea medicine and prednisone and are doing much better.

2BeCourageous was feeling thankful.
January 15, 2016 – 8:59 p.m.
I have been so unfair to my friends, whining about people who have chosen to no longer be in our lives when we have the most amazing and loving people in our lives every day. Many I have never met in person outside of Facebook, but I feel I have known many of you like we have known each other for years. Also, friends and family that are on this ride with us from the beginning, you are all amazing; my focus has been messed up and I apologize. We are so blessed to have you in our lives whether far or near, in person or online. I can't thank you enough for being there for us, and the prayers make such a difference. Thank you! Love and hugs!

2BeCourageous was feeling frustrated.
February 04, 2016 – 11:26 a.m.
Discouraged big time; my pain levels were down and physical therapy was making a big difference, then, yesterday, I woke up the way I started with this sciatica all the way down into my foot at a high level. I have too much to do to have this pain attack me again like this; it shuts me down and I can't have that. The first epidural shot is on next Monday. Don't know what to hope for, so many different responses from people [about] how it worked and didn't work for them.

2BeCourageous updated their status.
February 08, 2016 – 4:50 p.m.
Okay, here is today's adventure! Went to the pain clinic, an appointment at nine; was ready to leave when I was still waiting after ten. They had offered me sedation of Valium but I said no, thank you. So, I get in the

procedure room on the table and they start their numbing thing. I said, "You are numbing a lot of areas."

Doctor says, "Well, there are three injection spots we are going to do."

Me: "Wait, what? Three? I only signed up for one, I thought?!"

So, proceeding on, she says, "Let me know when you feel something in your leg!"

Me: "Huh? AHHH!"

They peeled me off the ceiling as I said, "Felt it!" The rest went okay, yeah it hurt some but not any more than the pain I walked in with, which I said was a 9; not putting 10 because they said that means you can't cope with it and are suicidal on their charts! (Laughing) I have learned never to even mention that word, it can land you in trouble. So, I came in a 9 and left a 2 on the pain scale. My whole side and leg were numb and I almost tipped over a few times. I felt sick afterward, not sure why, could have been no food or drink. Right now, I'm at a 1–2 range on pain and that is huge for me. Feeling hopeful about the injections but will no more tomorrow and as the week goes on. Next set of injections is next Monday the 15th. Just have to force myself not to overdo it.

2BeCourageous updated their status.
February 09, 2016 – 5:59 a.m.

Well, no sleep at all, started with a headache, I'm assuming from epidural shots I received yesterday in my back. Then Chet wouldn't sleep because I wasn't in bed, so he was up and down a dozen times and, one of his last times walking out to the living room, he was carrying our large George Foreman Grill that I had stored in our bedroom due to no room in the kitchen. So, we got into it over that and I got an "I hate you." He hasn't known who I was all day but he does know he hates me. Nice way to start the morning. I know it's not him saying that, it's the dementia, but it still hurts to hear it. His neurologist has called in trazodone for sleep and depression, so, if anyone has experience with that on dementia patients, please let me know what to possibly expect, knowing everyone reacts differently.

2BeCourageous was feeling emotional.
February 10, 2016 – 5:09 p.m.

I had to go to physical therapy today and then went grocery shopping after; Jake and Chessie stayed with Chet. When I got home, Jake told me Chet had a mental break, that he was in tears and upset because he couldn't help the people in the mirror and asked Jake and Chessie to help them and he got very upset. I knew, a few days ago, he wanted them to come out of there (the mirror). He has been talking to himself for several weeks in the mirror and it's been all good, it's his buddy, he says. Jake, on his own, covered the mirror with a blanket and said it's staying covered. I covered the bathroom ones too. I read in support groups about others having to cover or take mirrors down, but I thought we were going to be okay because he enjoyed the guy and other people in the mirror. I thought what's the harm? The other people being Jake or me when we would tell him it's our reflection, but he knew better and said it was friends of his buddy and he can't seem to tell that we and the reflections are the same people.

"Have I not commanded you? Be strong and courageous. Do not be frightened, and do not be dismayed, for the Lord your God is with you wherever you go."

JOSHUA 1:9 ESV

CHAPTER 18

CAN YOU SEE ME?

2BeCourageous updated their status.
February 10, 2016 – 10:27 p.m.

The first night Chet is on trazodone! He is snoring! I am loving that sound!

2BeCourageous updated their status
February 12, 2016 – 7:26 p.m.

My husband is very short with our four-year-old grandson; he will say get away from me to him, and go away and look real mean at him sometimes. He doesn't know who he is anymore, and children and their sudden loud noises upset my husband. I hear that's common. Braydon is still eager to help his grandpa and lead him to the bathroom or bring him to a chair and tell him to sit there. He knows his grandpa isn't perfect and has problems, but he helps him anyway out of love. Pretty good for a four-year-old.

2BeCourageous updated their status.
February 15, 2016 – 10:31 p.m.

I was pointing out the photos on the 2BeCourageous cover photo collage to Chet. I told him who each person was including himself. He laughed so hard like I was the one with dementia (I question myself some days) for saying that was him. He was not buying it tonight; that is not him! As much as I'd like to put more humor here, he didn't know who we were either. It's been some very hard three days for me, trying to come to terms with this. I've decided you just don't. There is nothing that will make me okay with it; there is nothing that will make me fully accept that one can be erased from one's memory including your own self. This disease is cruel and harsh and scary, creates sleepless nights for all.

2BeCourageous updated their status.
February 20, 2016 – 1:03 p.m.

By Chet's expression and gagging, I'm sure chewing a mouthful of medication tastes really bad! Yuck!

2BeCourageous updated their status.
February 27, 2016 – 10:04 p.m.

> Chet: "Wow! I'm at my home!"
> Me: "Welcome home? Where have you been?"
> Chet: "Yeah, I'm not sure, hmmm, somewhere."

Then he went back to not making a lot of sense that I could make out anyway. But he was glad to be home. He hasn't left the house physically for a week.

2BeCourageous was feeling discouraged.
March 01, 2016 – 11:58 p.m.

Not a happy camper. Physical therapy after ten weeks plus has not helped. After two sets of epidural injections, the second set lasted four to five days, has not helped. Pain has returned all from the low back all the way down the left leg into the ankle. The pain clinic doctor said today she feels I should have surgery. She said the MRI clearly shows the reason I'm in pain. She is going to run a nerve conduction test Thursday (Oh yeah, love those!) to see if it comes out positive, and, if it does, it's even one more reason to send my surgeon why I should have surgery. I don't even know what to pray for here but prayers are welcome. God will know.

2BeCourageous updated their status.
March 02, 2016 – 12:43 a.m.
I do not know how to even respond to my husband anymore. He cries several times a day and he can't tell me what is wrong. The things he tries to say make no sense, and he points to chairs and goes on about things but I'm just am not getting it. So, this frustrates him more. I write things out but it makes no sense to him. I keep telling him he is home and how we all love him and that he is safe here. He seems happy about that for maybe ten minutes. He cries hard, but no tears; he is very animated since going on the trazodone. He sleeps all night except to get up to pee. But he paces during the day and talks and talks but to himself. We tried to watch a movie with Jake the other night and Chet talked through the whole thing like they were real people in the room with him and he would shout at them on the TV.

He gets up early on his own and he dresses himself. He had on three shirts today that he got from the clean laundry I left on the kitchen table from the night before. He put on pants over his pajama pants.

This morning, I was so tired and got up and put the TV on for him in the living room and I lay back down. He stood at the end of the bed and screamed as loud as he could, "HELP ME!" Scared the crap out of me. I asked what was wrong and did he have to go to the bathroom? He said, "No, nothing is wrong." In a calm voice.

Last night, I gave him his night pills around six because he wouldn't settle down and relax and, by seven, he wanted to go home (bed) and he went right to sleep. Tonight, at 5:00 p.m., he was beyond restless, but

I tried to hold off as long as I could to give him his meds for the night. The trazodone seems to stop this restlessness and crying. I need to write his doctor about this, I guess. I don't want him zoned out all day ... but I don't want him miserable crying either. Life is getting harder to figure out.

2BeCourageous updated their status.
March 04, 2016 – 4:05 a.m.

Trazodone has made a big difference at night for sleep. Today, he was yelling out in the living room by himself around 7:30 a.m. I went to bed at 5:00 a.m.; he cried at least ten times today. Even when the entire family was over for dinner, he paces all day and talks to himself and tries to explain to us that the people need help and he can't help them. He screams, "Help me!" and cries. He is so stressed and restless. He called me stupid several times this morning and was so angry with me because I wasn't helping the others.

I have written his doctor and requested something for him to calm him during the day. He struggles to swallow his pills now, and I know swallowing can be an issue in late stages. He has chewed them in the past, and I only let him take one at a time now. It's hard to instruct him because he drops them or puts them in his drink, not getting what I want of him. He chewed a time-release capsule the other day. I finally got liquid in his mouth to down it. I'm tired.

I wouldn't let Chessie and Braydon come over today until we got Chet calmed, but it didn't last after they got here. How do you get a four-year-old to understand this? He took Chet's hand and led him to the couch and said to him, "Sit here, Papa." He will lead him to the bathroom saying, "Follow me, Papa, this way." At times, Chet is mean to him, mean attitude, grumpy towards him. That breaks my heart to see that. But Chessie wants to be here with us and I love her for that! Both my kids, age twenty-one now, are very supportive and loving and want to be here; my son in law also comes over when he isn't working. I am blessed to have them all.

2BeCourageous was feeling frustrated.
March 06, 2016 – 3:49 a.m.

Well, it's 3:15 a.m., I need sleep but already worried about the morning when it all starts again. He is talking to photos on the wall now because he can see his reflection in the glass and his trapped friend is in there! Same with the storm door on the front door and the car windows. Crying and saying he is bad and he is in trouble. Pacing, crying.

He didn't want to get into the car with us at the bank while I was applying for a loan. Jake brought him in to go to the bathroom, and he was all agitated coming out and refusing to go with us, not knowing us.

Today, I went out with my daughter and her friend for a few hours and Jake called me three times because he couldn't calm his dad down, and Jake has been the one with the magic touch with him. Both of my kids tell me, "That's not our father; we do not know him anymore," and it breaks my heart because he is no longer the man I married. He is still Chet, just not the one we knew. My hope is that he is in there, but this horrible disease has hidden him away. We are strangers to him, and he is a stranger in a way to us.

I've argued with his neurologist about medication. I said he needs more than an antidepressant; he needs something to calm him and his paranoid or psychotic thinking. I have twice now given him trazodone during the day; it helps some to bring him down. The doctor said, "I don't want him to be tired," so she won't order it for twice a day. Instead, she wants to stop cold turkey [the] Effexor and, the next day, start Paxil. It's another antidepressant. I said, "He isn't depressed, he is gone! And, at this point, who gives a crap if he is tired during the day? It's better than crying and pacing!" I told her we are about the quality of life because we know quantity is not long, and it is not quality thinking people are trapped and it's your fault you can't save them. Then cry hourly and not sit down to rest! That is not quality! I said, "The trazodone helped. You are ignoring that part because you don't want him tired during the day?" I requested what I said I would never put him on and that's Seroquel. I've been on it. So, now when I get done being ticked off, I will go pick up the Paxil and cold turkey my husband off Effexor (Been there done that, so I know!) and hope the brain zaps (withdrawal symptom, well-documented) do not make him go over what we can handle!

One of my bad qualities is I need to be in control. Well, that is impossible with Alzheimer's.

2BeCourageous updated their status.
March 08, 2016 – 11:46 a.m.

Last night was his first time on Paxil and off Effexor—one day. The doctor said it is in the same drug group, so there isn't a withdrawal from Effexor, so I will try it and see. But he has so many other health issues. I'm taking him into the primary care physician to see if he has a UTI (urinary tract infection). He is beside himself, telling us he is dead and asking me if I can see him, and telling us how evil he is, and I can tell he isn't feeling good physically. His stomach looked bloated yesterday but not so much today, and he gets full halfway through a meal. I will tell her (the primary care physician) about the trazadone and that the neuro switched him to Paxil. I'm worn out with him and it's not even noon yet!

2BeCourageous was feeling concerned.
March 08, 2016 – 10:29 p.m.

Chet has a very bad bladder infection and he was running a fever, and he still is. I know this is common in Alzheimer's patients; I do not know why, though, they tend to get UTIs, but I know from being in support groups that the infections can cause more confusion and affect them mentally, and, once the infection clears up, so does some of the confusion! I'm so hoping his mental state will clear up! Aricept and Namenda do cause urinary retention, though, but they won't take him off the drugs. I also mentioned his stomach was bloated yesterday and he is having trouble eating; just can't eat as much, gets full eating half of what he usually does, and complains how uncomfortable he is after eating.

The PCP put him on ten days of Levaquin. She said she can't do anything about the continued blood in the urine, and felt it was from the kidney mass and not the stricture surgery from January 12th. That should have been healed by now and that he needs to see his urologist sooner than April. He should have the repeat CT scan of the tumor on his kidney sooner considering his symptoms. I told her I had called the urologist two or three times now about the blood in his urine from two weeks after the surgery, and the last time about two weeks ago. He keeps saying it's not unusual for blood to be in the urine this far out of surgery and we will see what the follow-up CAT scan shows [in] the beginning of April.

I think (guessing here) the problem is the urologist isn't sure how to proceed. I know he thinks it's cancer and his patient is in late-stage Alzheimer's and it's in a spot they can't reach to freeze it. Chet didn't handle the simpler stricture procedure and refused to cooperate before surgery, and then after surgery with the catheter. How would he ever handle having a kidney removed because that sounded like the only option? I'm thinking maybe moving him back to Vanderbilt for the kidney issue. Not sure, will call tomorrow and request a sooner CAT scan but I know he wants to wait to see if the mass is growing.

He has been healthy over the years, and BAM! Brain, heart, and kidneys and bladder and he doesn't complain of pain verbally. If I had an infection like he does now, I'd be crying .... Oh my gosh! He has been crying nonstop, saying he is bad and evil and has done bad things, but that's it. I wonder if that's his pain coming out. Because of his communication struggles, he can't tell us outright. I should have known! I never connected the crying until this moment. Please pray the antibiotics kick in fast and give him relief, and pray this has caused the psychotic behavior and it will cease once the UTI is healed.

Oh, I told her (PCP) about the neurologist putting him on Paxil and off Effexor, she said GOOD! My brain went blank when I tried to tell her about trazodone working during the day; that dang name would not come to me for anything! She's trying to guess and I could not come up with it. What the heck! I'm scaring myself!

2BeCourageous updated their status.
March 09, 2016 – 11:17 p.m.
Well, day two on antibiotics for his bladder infection and no change yet. Day three on Paxil and off Effexor and he is up and down, up and down from bed again; finally sleeping now! Shhhh!

He was cute yesterday. I needed to change my top and he was in the bedroom with me, and I pulled my top off and he looked shocked and turned around and stood to face the corner. After a few seconds, I said, "What are you doing?"

He turns around looking embarrassed and says, "I like you and all, you are very nice but I can't!"

I said, "I'm just changing, and we are married going on twenty-five years."

He says, "Noooo, really?"

I forget I'm living with my husband who doesn't know me most of the time. I'm living with a stranger. He sure wasn't that shy when we met! (Laughing) I made him smile today, singing to him how much I loved him; it is hard getting him to smile nowadays.

2BeCourageous was feeling thankful.
March 10, 2016 – 5:31 p.m.
Wow, what a difference three days of antibiotics make; I believe it's the antibiotics for the bladder infection over the Paxil! No crying today, no "I want to kill myself," and no "I'm dead" or can you see me questions. A kind of normal day, as normal as it can get in the Alzheimer's/FTD World. Praise!

2BeCourageous updated their status.
March 11, 2016 – 9:40 p.m.
It was a fairly good day, Chet was crying in bed this morning before we got up and couldn't tell me why, but was okay the rest of the day. I've been giving him AZO for relief of the bladder pain, and it turns your pee orange and that has stopped the panic of him seeing blood in his urine;

he would freak when he saw the blood but is okay with the orange pee because it's medicine. It also stains when he misses the toilet.

He has been enjoying going outside in our seventy-degree days and picking up sticks in the yard; huge yard, lots of sticks fall from the trees, and, when he runs out, we sneak more sticks out and toss them about for him. I know, my bad! (Laughing) But it keeps him busy, and he just does it on his own and doesn't have episodes outside when he is busy. Now I know, for my children, this brings back memories of the Easter Beaver. (Laughing)

When my twins were like three and four, we had a stuffed toy beaver and Chet developed a story of the Easter Beaver. He told the kids that the Easter Beaver was going to bring them goodies in a basket, but only if they picked up sticks in the yard and made a pile for the Easter Beaver to make his home out of. So, breaking child labor laws, our kids picked up lots of sticks in the yard. We had woods in front of our farm and behind our farm; no shortage of sticks. (Laughing) Ah, the memories. Hugs and love to you all, your comments and support mean so much to me!

2BeCourageous updated their status.
March 12, 2016 – 10:51 a.m.
Bad idea to give someone who can't hit the toilet AZO! Bad me, dumb me! I now have orange grout in the floor, orange walls, and orange toilet; nothing, I'm sure, made it into the toilet. Ugh! Maybe I will redo this bathroom too now … in orange … (laughing).

2BeCourageous updated their status.
March 24, 2016 – 11:17 p.m.
I am so blessed to have two understanding and loving children that allow me to walk out of the house and leave for an hour or two when my emotions are spilling over with frustration from an ongoing poopy day (literally). I just needed to walk it off in Walmart, Easter shopping for my grandson. Thank you, Jake and Chessie, for always being there for me! You two always amaze me how wonderful you both are. I think you get it from your dad! By the way, shopping with heightened emotion isn't a

good idea, my bipolar type two was trying to take over. I did put about half of the stuff back on the shelves that were in my cart … not the right shelves but, at least, it all didn't make it to checkout.

2BeCourageous updated their status.
April 05, 2016 – 10:08 p.m.

Angels among us.

To the lady that was working in the Walmart today in Smyrna, TN, I did not get your name. I want to thank you for your kindness and what you did for my husband and myself. My husband with Alzheimer's had a BM accident in his pants in the middle of Walmart while he and I and Jake were shopping. It went through the Depend and all over his pants. I took him into the ladies' room and into the handicap stall, knowing he had soaked through his jeans and hoped I could somehow clean him up enough to ride home in my (new) car! A cleaning lady was in the bathroom but I took him in any way. She figured out what was going on quickly by the smell and my panicked attitude. She gave me paper towels and a plastic bag.

Then, another employee came in and started talking to me through the door saying she went through this with her mom in a store and understood. She asked me if I needed her to get him some pants. I said I don't have an extra pair with us. She said what size and I told her medium. She was gone about ten minutes while I cleaned my husband up, she came back and said she got pajama pants in a large; they were bagged with a receipt and I said, "You paid for them?" (I had planned on it after I got him cleaned.) I started to say, "Let me … " I wanted to say "pay you" but she cut me off and said, "Do not worry about it!" She left. Thank you from the bottom of my heart. God bless you! Thank you to the lady cleaning also, she was very kind. Having someone approach us that has been through it meant so much to me, makes you feel less alone in this battle.

"And the prayer of faith will save the sick, and the Lord shall raise him up. And if he has committed sins, they shall be forgiven him."

JAMES 5:15-16 KJV

CHAPTER 19

THREE HOSPITALS IN TWENTY-FOUR HOURS

2BeCourageous updated their status.
April 10, 2016 – 3:28 a.m.

It's been a hard week; I haven't felt good, I don't write much about my personal health struggles much here on my 2BeCourageous page. I guess because I write so much about it on my personal page I forget not everyone on here are friends with me on my personal page. I'm having surgery on Tuesday, the 12th, at 7:30 a.m. for a ruptured disc that is lying on my sciatic nerve and affects my whole left side, from my low back to my foot and all in between. I've been battling this pain since October. Please pray for success. I had to stop the anti-inflammatory medications all this week before surgery and, man, oh man, the pain doubled. So, I know they were helping some. But I had to up the pain pills. Surgery is outpatient if all goes well.

I took Chet back to the PCP to check for another UTI because he was crying again and very agitated and mean/rude. He was crying in the doctor's office exam room hard, and I was glad because she could see for herself because, other times, we go and I say well he is doing this and that and he sits there and makes jokes or faces or does nothing. He always sings to her. He had no infection, which disappointed me in a way because that was my answer to fix him because, last time, when he did have one and got treated, his mind and behavior improved very quickly. She does think he is having bladder spasms, though, so he is on meds for that briefly to see if it helps. So, our PCP made the decision in which the neurologist has been putting off, and she put him on Zyprexa 5 mg, an antipsychotic. She felt the Paxil wasn't helping, plus he developed a vocal tic from it, we think, where he goes "HMM, HMMM" over and over, and I can tell he isn't just doing it on purpose to annoy me! I have to wean him off the Paxil.

We were sitting in the waiting room at the doctor's and he was being difficult, wanting to leave and talking loud. Much of the time, you cannot understand his sentences, but, today, he was speaking clear when he said, "I want to sit over there," pointing to the couch where a lady was sitting by herself.

He started to get up and I pulled his arm back down and said, "Sit with me."

He said angrily, "Don't you touch me again!"

I said, "Sorry, just sit with me."

He says, "I want to sit there, she is prettier." Needless to say, this made the lady very uncomfortable and she got up and moved to the other side of the room, and it didn't make me feel the best either. Yup. Thank you all for the kind support you show us and please add a prayer for my surgery on Tuesday.

2BeCourageous replied.
April 10, 2016 – 7:36 p.m.
I am aware what some antipsychotics can do to elderly dementia patients, and they seem to affect Lewy body more so, and Chet does not have

Lewy body. He has early-onset Alzheimer's/FTD; he also is not elderly. The drug the PCP put him on was the exact drug his neuro talked about putting him on but wanted to try the Paxil first, and they are very aware of the effects it can have on the patient; we discussed it with the neuro a while back and I brought it up to the PCP. He needs relief of the living nightmare he is in, and we need relief also.

2BeCourageous was feeling nervous.
April 11, 2016 – 10:57 p.m.
I'm worn out and starting to question home care. I just need to feel better and have high hopes on surgery in the morning to stop the pain. I know I will have pain from the surgery, but getting rid of the sciatic pain I've dealt with the last six months should help my attitude and mood. Getting off the pain pills, I know, will help my mood also. I must wean off them. We will be leaving in a few hours for the hospital; please keep us all in your prayers.

2BeCourageous updated their status.
April 12, 2016 – 4:41 p.m.
I am home! I hurt big time! There is no comfortable position right now. I thought lying on my stomach would be best, it's the worst! The pain continues to get worse in my lower back, but I was told it would hurt. I went there with about level 8 out of 10 pain in the butt down the leg. That is about an 8 right now; it is hard to tell. They told me the leg area may still hurt for a week or two because the nerve was compressed and needs time to return to normal, and not to get upset if it does hurt.

I know this sounds stupid but, for some reason, I thought they would cut alongside the spine, but they cut right on it. Silly me! I will copy and paste this into a new post also. Misty gave up her day to be with me; she is a wonderful friend! Thank you, my bonus daughter. Thank you, Jake and Chessie, for being here at home for me and taking care of me and watching daddy today I felt at ease leaving, knowing you guys had it handled …. Love you guys!

2BeCourageous updated their status.

April 14, 2016 – 2:39 p.m.

I need help for Jake; he is trying to take care of me and Chet who just had a BM accident all over the entire bathroom. Jake is gone, he went to the pharmacy to get me medication for spasms, and Chet's in the bathroom screaming, "Help me! Help me!" I couldn't get up because my sciatic nerve and muscles go into a major spasm down my leg when I get up. I have been screaming and crying half the night and most of the late morning with uncontrollable nerve spasms. Pain level when that happens is a 22. This is too much for Jake to deal with, he is throwing Chet's clothes out and the rug out because Chet used his clothes to try and wipe things down; and his shoes, he ground it all into the rug. I have new meds in me. Hopefully, it will work. Please pray for us; I can't deal right now, I'm calling Chet's case manager at the health insurance to see our options.

2BeCourageous updated their status.

April 15, 2016 – 10:30 a.m.

Made it through the night without a nerve spasm attack down my left side. My friend Misty's idea of setting an alarm clock to keep me on track on medications has helped immensely. I have never been down on my back—and side—this long at home, but I'm following orders. My son refuses to let me up unless it's to go to the bathroom, which triggers sciatica spasms. But he talked to my surgeon last night and he called in steroids and Valium along with the other meds I already have—gabapentin, oxycodone every four hours, and a muscle relaxer and all my normal meds I take. I can't see too straight and I'm a little out of it. Jake DeBoer is keeping me on track. Jake has a plan to start getting me up slowly to sit in the living room tonight and more and more each day.

I called my case manager who is now Chet's case manager also through Humana. She is sending me a week of frozen dinners for one person, but it helps, and sending Chet a home care nurse to evaluate his needs and come out several times a week is what they feel is needed. No cost to me.

I got up to go to the bathroom four hours ago with no spasm down the leg. I was so scared because they last around twenty to thirty minutes, and I'm frozen in pain the entire time with me screaming and crying. It's like a Charley horse times twenty in pain. I've never experienced that level of pain before. Not even labor hurt like this! What a relief not to have it this time! Hope this means things are looking up. My poor son has been amazing. Chet cries and carries on when I cry during those attacks, so Jake gets a double whammy of us. Chessie has been over, helping when she can, but Braydon, my grandson, has been home sick, so she is taking care of my little red.

2BeCourageous updated their status.
April 18, 2016 – 5:50 p.m.
I woke up to Jake asking, "Who ate the last half of the cake?"

I said, "Not me," which left the guilty party, Mr. Diabetic himself, Chester Dale, with a sugar level up in the upper 300s to prove his guilt, and, somehow, the smile on his face spelled guilty!

2BeCourageous updated their status.
April 22, 2016 – 5:12 p.m.
I do not like life right now. Chet had to take fifteen prednisone pills and a couple of Benadryl in a twelve-hour period during the night because he is allergic to the IVP dye for CAT scans. Well, most likely, this has turned him into a complete mean and unruly person today. Pacing nonstop, yelling, and just hateful. I feared the drugs would react negatively, but they couldn't do a detailed CAT scan without the IVP dye. So, now, we all suffer for it. He is close to being committed, hoping the drugs wear off soon. Hoping it's the drugs also that is causing this behavior.

Heidi DeBoer updated her status.
April 23, 2016 – 6:44 p.m.
Yesterday, around five-ish, Chet and I lay down in bed for a nap. Jake saw we were both sleeping and he needed a part for the lawn tractor, so he ran

up to Lowe's really quick. When Jake got back, he drove into the driveway and saw Chet and Emmy from right across the street sitting on the front porch steps and Chet crying. While I was asleep, Chet got up and went outside into the driveway and started yelling, "Help! Help!" Emmy was outside and ran over. She knew he has Alzheimer's but I didn't know her well, and she said she yelled into the house to see if I was okay but was scared to go in. God bless neighbors like Emmy and her husband. I slept through it all; I felt horrible! I went over and thanked her later after I got myself together enough to think straight.

Jake just went to a one-year memorial party for Chessie's father-in-law who passed suddenly last April, and he said to call him if anything goes wrong and he'd be right home. HA! Diarrhea explosion everywhere; what the heck are adult diapers good for if they pour out the legs? I did not call Jake, didn't want to ruin his night, and I'm surely going to hell for my foul mouth! I just want to heal. I just want my leg pain to stop; I just want off the pain pills because they are a big cause of my foul mouth, I'm sure. I just want to be able to handle all this. I just don't want to feel like quitting on him. I just want to feel good about life again. I just want to find things to joke about and laugh about again. That's me, not this horrible person I feel I am turning into. I need to put it back in God's hands.

Heidi DeBoer updated her status.
April 27, 2016 – 11:54 p.m.
Well, after a horrible week last week, things have calmed down with Chet, and the steroids are getting out of his system and never will he get them again! Holy moly! He gets very angry easily and, if we can't figure a reason for it, we ignore it and get his mind onto something else. The Gaither Vocal Band has lost its appeal to him, and I'm not sure if the swearing belonged in some of those songs, but he has added and rewrote them today. On every song, he then thanked God when each song was over. He was one to never use the F word, but it has been in his vocabulary a lot lately. Stress, I guess, and his brain changing him into a different person. We are working on getting respite care to give us a couple of hours

here and there out while someone stays with him. His case manager from Humana was over today and said I could possibly get vouchers to pay health care places to come and sit with him for an hour or two at a time. Positive for today is I moved a little easier today, and God is good even during our bad times. He is good!

2BeCourageous updated their status.
May 02, 2016 – 5:16 p.m.
Tomorrow, Chet has kidney stone laser surgery to blast away a very large kidney stone that's giving him trouble. He is very agitated and got out of hand at 4:00 a.m. We went for pre-op paperwork today, so I warned them I don't know how he will act so they are prepared. He needs either more medication to calm him or new meds. Pray for a successful and calm day tomorrow; I already said no prednisone and no catheter!

2BeCourageous shared Heidi DeBoer's post.
May 03, 2016 – 1:24 p.m.
We are here waiting in Room 8 in the surgery center for him to go back. His doctor just came in and said,it's an hour surgery or less; he said they'll put a stent in and, if they can't get into where the stone is, then he will have to come back in a week to go up and get the stone blasted. I did not know this and didn't understand it either. But he said it's a 5% chance they can't get up there. They won't put a string on the stent because of the like-lihood of him pulling it out. Pray they do it all today; I don't want to put him through this again. The stress lately is too much, especially the last two days he has done things I'd never think he would do, so keep those prayers coming!

2BeCourageous shared Heidi DeBoer's post.
May 03, 2016 – 1:26 p.m.
Chet is in the recovery room, waking up, and everything went great. They got the kidney stone blasted and put a stent in. We are going to try to have it taken out in a week in the doctor's office if Chet will tolerate having that

done to him. The doctor said he really doesn't want to get kicked in the face. Otherwise, he must be put under again to have it taken out, but we opted to try in the doctor's office first. He should be brought back here to the room in a half hour and we wait, I'm not sure how long, to see how he is and then go home. I will be honest, I didn't want him to come home today; I just wanted him to stay overnight to let the anesthesia wear off here. The doctor reconfirmed that we are leaving the mass alone and will watch it for now

2BeCourageous shared Heidi DeBoer's post.
May 03, 2016 – 1:49 p.m.
Update on Chet: He is in a lot of pain; they had given him a hydroco-done but that didn't help, so they gave him morphine. They are keeping him for twenty-three hours, I guess it's still considered outpatient, and it's only okay due to pain management being the reason used. Like late-stage Alzheimer's didn't seem to matter, but the nurses and doctor seem very understanding, its insurance that is fussy. At first, the nurses and doctor kept saying patients who have the procedure go home, and I kept saying he is not a normal patient, just look and listen to him! He needs more help through this! I won! But I might have to get his home meds, depending on what the insurance says. They said they would bring in a sitter tonight if I want to go home and sleep. I'm not sure what to do; I'm scared to leave him and feel guilty to leave him. They will never keep him in bed later; I'm scared they will strap him in. I'm so confused on what to do, and tears come all morning easily! I think I'm the one that needs to be admitted somewhere! Sigh.

2BeCourageous updated their status.
May 04, 2016 – 8:08 a.m.
I got back to the hospital about 6:15 a.m. or so. Jake got home around 10:00 or 11:00 last night from a film rehearsal, and we ended up talking until 3:00 a.m. One thing he and I do well is to talk to wee morning hours. Needless to say, I didn't sleep much. But did get a feeling of not stressing

those few hours, worrying what Chet was constantly doing. He tried to get up every forty-five minutes, trying to pee and get out of bed. He can't wake up this morning and, when he tries to get up, he seems very weak and so out of it. I have asked them to make sure they walk him before sending him home, so we know he can walk right. He does not know me right now; he is so out of it. I'm exhausted, my fault, but we are addicted to talking in the wee hours of the morning. No idea when they will kick Chet out.

2BeCourageous updated their status.
May 04, 2016 – 2:13 p.m.
Oh my freaking whatever! I'm so mad I don't even know what to do right now! Chet had a laser blast on a kidney stone done. I asked to please keep him, he doesn't come off anesthesia well and he is in major pain, and he has late-stage Alzheimer's, which makes everything worse. They got permission to keep him for twenty-three to twenty-four hours. I got there at 6:15 a.m. or so and he was out of it, and they were just encouraging him to pee his pants/diaper instead of using the guy pee cup thing you hold. They had drugged him several times to keep him calm in bed, so he would stop trying to get out of it. He was practically unresponsive, had to feed him breakfast; he couldn't hold his head up. I asked several times, please make sure he can walk or I will never get him in the house. Never once did they get him up and, at noon, they said okay, he can go now. I called home and the kids were not home and not answering their cell phones. I said, "You are sending him home like this? He can't hold his head up!"

They dressed him, put him in a chair, and he just laid his head on the table in front of the chair. I said, "I can't get him in the house, I just had back surgery, no one is home."

They said, "He would wake up more; you can get the car."

I was so mad I could not hold the tears back. It took a guy and a girl to struggle to get him in the car. He looked dead slouched forward, so they leaned the seat back! We got home; we have a handicap ramp in the back that came with the house. I had a wheelchair in the shed from when

I broke my ankle in 2013. I got that, our driveway is gravel. In tears, I went across the street to my neighbor who is a healthcare nurse aide and works in long-term care. Thank God, she was home and came to help me. She did it all; she had a geri belt to help get him up, and we pushed him up the ramp, and she got him into bed for me! What an angel Emmy is.

I'm just so mad over it how this all happened! Needed to vent and brag about my angel of a neighbor. She was the one that came to Chet's rescue when he was in the driveway yelling HELP! I'm exhausted mentally. Sorry for always being negative, just writing it like it is! This is all due to health insurance!

2BeCourageous updated their status.
May 04, 2016 – 9:14 p.m.
I had Chet in a wheelchair most of the afternoon, strapped in, and he started saying, "Help me, help me," exactly like the last time we saw his grandmother in a nursing home. He could not hold his head up most of the day; we started helping him walk, both Jake and me together or Jake alone. Got him in bed and he tried getting up and we caught him in time to help him, but, later, we hear a crash and he had fallen and hit his head hard on the wire dog kennel cage that is at the end of our bed. A small lump and scratch on his head. He is mad we help him and makes fists or slaps my hands trying to give him pills. I will be making calls tomorrow to complain! He could walk fine when he went in for the kidney stone blast.

2BeCourageous updated their status.
May 05, 2016 – 5:14 p.m.
Both Chet and I slept in the den last night on the sectional couch, he at one end me on the other. We got up a few times for the bathroom and Jake got right up to help. Chet and I slept to about 3:00 in the afternoon. Jake and Chessie went out and did a beginning of the month grocery shopping while we slept, and I guess Jake was hungry—they brought back a lot! (Laughing)

Chet is walking again this afternoon with a little help and asking to pee when he has to go and making it there. He sat at the kitchen table to eat stuffed shells that Chessie made and brought over! Yummy! So, Chet is doing better, just worn out.

I think I'm having a breakdown; I keep crying every time I talk about what happened. Thought I had myself together and called my mom back who called earlier and I just started crying telling her, and I know it upsets her when I'm upset but I couldn't help it. I also called the hospital to complain and cried, and I called the surgeon's office to make an in-office appointment to remove the stent without a string on it; he isn't sure he can do it only because he doesn't know if Chet will tolerate it since there is no string on it. I also complained to the office. I wish we would have done this at Vandy instead of Stonecrest where we went for the surgery. I wrote the hospital on Facebook messenger and got a response and an investigation into what happened. The head nurse said she would get back to me. She called me to tell me there would be no charge for that stay and was very nice to me. I got a letter stating that also, no charge.

2BeCourageous updated their status.
May 08, 2016 – 10:44 p.m.
Good night, friends; thank you for the love and prayers, which gets us through hour by hour. Chet has an appointment on Tuesday to get the stent out, first try will be in office, pray for that to work. Otherwise, its anesthesia again in the hospital! Also, he will be either going to our primary care physician or neurologist office this week; appointment not made yet to get a referral for hospice. But our nurse case manager from Humana Insurance who calls us a few times a month, she is mine and Chet's, which is nice now. After talking it out with her, we are going to have Chet evaluated for hospice care in the home. HOSPICE DOES NOT MEAN END-OF-LIFE CARE! He is not in the final stage but late stage, and hospice will come in and help with him if he qualifies. So, we are just seeing if he qualifies and that will be a huge help for us!

2BeCourageous was thanking God.

May 10, 2016 – 12:39 p.m.

PRAISE! Chet went to the urologist's office today and had the procedure to take out the stent with no string attached. So, the doctor had to go up and get it from the kidney area with a scope. I gave Chet one of his pain pills from his surgery that he has not even needed anymore to help him and everything went well! YES! No problem getting it. The urologist acted surprised that Chet was released like he was and said doctor so and so was supposed to see him. I said, "Well, no one saw him."

He said, "Well, he would come early."

I said, "I was there before 6:30 a.m. and the sitter said no one was in."

The doctor kept changing the subject after that, like avoiding to listen to what happened. But praises for today, Chet did well!

Heidi DeBoer updated her status.

May 14, 2016 – 9:10 p.m.

You know your old friend, fibro, is back when every inch of your body hurts to touch. Well, hello, old friend, competing with sciatica today? Thank goodness, I have a God bigger than both of you, so crawl under a rock!

Heidi DeBoer updated her status.

May 16, 2016 – 11:05 p.m.

Well, I never dreamed that my husband's snoring would be a welcomed sound! I used to punch him lightly in the arm years ago to wake him up and he would say, "What are you doing?" I'd say, "I didn't do anything, you must be dreaming." I know, I know. I'm bad! Now, his snoring wins over his wandering the house the last two weeks every night. Snore away, baby!

2BeCourageous updated their status.

May 19, 2016 – 8:26 p.m.

I have the nicest neighbor ever. Emmy and her husband live across the street; I brought her flowers and thanked her and returned the geri belt she let me use to help get Chet up and down that day.

Today, she came to the door and had bought Chet a package of Depend and some disposable bed pads. That was so nice and huge help because we are out of money this month. These extras of diapers and pads and other medical things are adding up. What a huge help this was and what a sweet lady! I hope we can become good friends. God is good!

2BeCourageous updated their status.
May 21, 2016 – 10:05 p.m.

Chet was having a hard time on Thursday and he was pounding walls and tables and cussing (not the old him at all). So, I knew we were dealing with a UTI or something bladder-related. Got him in the same day and he had blood in urine, but no infection. She felt he needed to be on the hydrocodone the urologist gave him after laser blast of a kidney stone a couple of weeks back. I didn't have him on it because he displayed no pain and would say he didn't have any. She felt the blasted pieces were probably passing. She also wanted him back on AZO that helps bladder spasms and turned pee and carpets orange forever!

Friday morning, Chet woke up leaning towards his right side. Wasn't sure why, thought he might be too drugged from the hydrocodone (narcotic) or his antipsychotic, Zyprexa. Jake and I did all the stroke tests we knew and he passed all of them. My friend came over and said it could be ministroke and came over to observe him, but also felt it could be medication. She talked to an ER nurse who thought it was ministroke. I took him off the hydrocodone last night. Still leaning today, so I emailed the neurologist at Vandy, saying we need to be seen next week ASAP.

I went to a graduation party just to wish the graduate well and not stay long while Jake stayed with Chet. Saw my friend, Judy, there; I told her what was going on and she said he could have an ear infection. That made so much sense! Our PCP is open until four on Saturdays and I raced home to get Chet and called them. They arranged and switched patients around, so Chet could see his PCP instead of someone else. I love these ladies that work there! He has an ear infection in his right ear, red and fluids in it. His PCP is the best. She said, though, it still could be a TIA and, if so, they will watch him until we find the reason. He is on antibiotics for the ear infection. Will be getting him in for testing hopefully Monday at Vanderbilt. Thank you for all the love and prayers and support.

– Heidi at 2BeCourageous

Update: Sunday, he is doing better mood-wise but getting sick, coughing and ear infection and sinus now.

2BeCourageous updated their status.
May 23, 2016 – 3:39 a.m.
I've never had bags under my eyes, I'm so tired and he just peed on my dresser and carpet again. Orange! Last night, he never slept, up and down all night. I hate this, there are times I dislike him but I know he can't help it. Do not judge me and my feelings; if you have not done this with a dementia person 24/7, or part-time even, you have no idea!

Heidi DeBoer updated her status.
May 24, 2016 – 9:42 a.m.
Went to see my surgeon yesterday. Now the story is it can take a year for the nerve to regenerate and heal. Funny he never mentioned that presurgery; he said I should have no pain when I wake up from surgery! Well, it feels worse some days. So, now I have another scar to add to me; what's one more right? Plus, I hurt the same and worse some days. He said the nerve is free; they removed a bone to get to it and filed down bone spurs around it and took the bulge off it. He said they could get an instrument down around it, so it has plenty of room.

2BeCourageous shared Heidi DeBoer's post.

May 26, 2016 – 7:43 a.m.

Here is your entertainment for this evening! Ginger and Fred! LOL aka … us.

May 26, Chet is feeling good, good enough to dance to the Glen Miller Band in the living room with me that we got on video. This dance will always be a cherished memory, it was so fun for me and he seemed to enjoy it also.

This reminded me of our early days when we would travel to Lowell, IN and go to the big barn dance they used to have there. We both would be dressed in our Western attire and we would dance the two-step or try anyways (laughing), but we would be in each other's arms on the slow dances and it was like we were the only ones there, caught up in each other. It was so romantic.

Heidi DeBoer updated her status.

May 26, 2016 – 4:41 p.m.

I found one of Chet's diplomas while looking for the title of the van so I could scrap the van. He got his pastor's diploma, a three-year program, at the time back in the late '70s, and this college, Grand Rapids School of Bible and Music, years later became part of Cornerstone University. He later went back to Cornerstone University and received his Bachelor's degree in Organizational Leadership in the '90s. He got caught up in the Christian bookstore industry, designing the interiors and shelving units. I wonder what his life would have been like if he had gone [with] his first career choice. I wonder if we would have even met. God's path isn't always what we plan; I'm glad mine led to Chet. He had decided after graduating with a pastor's diploma that talking in front of crowds was not for him.

2BeCourageous updated their status.

May 29, 2016 – 11:10 p.m.

The change in just a couple weeks' time in my husband is heart-crushing. He stands motionless and stares at the ground. He sits with his head down, leaving us wondering if he is awake or asleep. He is having trouble feeding himself and eating less; he says he doesn't like the food. He is on a new medication since Saturday and was taken off another medication, both antipsychotics. He is calmer but now active again.

I cut the morning one in half today to see if it would help but it didn't. He was out of hand, pacing all night long and all day and mad! He punched Jake in the stomach while Jake was talking on the phone. Jake said it didn't hurt but he knew Chet meant for it to hurt! Jake said he likes the calmness. We haven't had calmness in a very long time and I can see why he says that. But it makes me so sad. I look at him and see a man trapped inside, trying to get out like the people he saw in the mirror. He had to rescue them; perhaps it really was himself he saw and knew he needed rescuing but it was too late. He is completely incontinent now for urine and bowel; just in a few days that happened, not asking to go anymore.

Jake and I will sit for hours at night and just talk. We make each other laugh. I told him in a late night conversation that people will tell me Chet really does know me in his heart, and he really is the same person inside. Being the straightforward person Jake is, he tells it like it is. He said, "Mom, the heart has no capabilities of memory; it all comes from the brain." He said, "These dementias kill the brain cells; once they are gone, they are gone, dead. He can't remember because that part of the brain or some of the cells there are dying or dead."

It's common sense to my son. For me, you just need to hang on to the heart theory of having memories and feelings and not mention the brain for sanity reasons, to make it hurt less. False hopes, but, if that is what a person needs to believe, what does it hurt? I think it helps us through these diseases.

Ear infection must be going away; the right side lean is almost gone. We should get his MRI results Tuesday or Wednesday. He did good, he listened and laid still for the entire thing with earplugs in.

Two of our pastors came to visit us this week. It did my heart good!

I needed that. It made everything good again in my heart. Thanks for reading my page. Hugs.

2BeCourageous updated their status.
June 03, 2016 – 5:42 p.m.
Chet is in ER at Vanderbilt University Medical Center; I am a wreck and very sad right now. They have him in a hall, you know, royal treatment, and won't let Jake sit with me with Chet because only one is allowed in the hall; he won't get a room upstairs until after ten to eleven at night, if even then. Chet can't stand on his own, can't eat on his own, can't walk on his own; he is drooling and he can't hold his head up. I believe the Haldol antipsychotic medication did this too him. I hate these drugs! I am beside myself; I'm just losing it. I think everything building wants to come out right now. Jake is back with Chet.

Heidi DeBoer updated her status.
June 04, 2016 – 9:21 a.m.
I am at the hospital with Chet, he is the same; they think it was the Haldol medication or his Alzheimer's took a major step. They are keeping him off his medication to see if he can get back to the baseline where he was.

Heidi DeBoer updated her status.
June 04, 2016 5:12 p.m.
There wasn't much change today, he can't eat and he is opening his eyes but only for seconds. He tries to say something but he is so weak, nothing will come out. He just sleeps unless nurses YELL REALLY LOUD AT HIM to get a response from him. Every test has come back normal, and he hasn't had Haldol since Thursday night. They are talking short-term rehab here in La Vergne or Smyrna to help us know how to move him and lift him, so we don't hurt ourselves and to try to get him back on his feet or back to baseline as they call it. They admit him to the hospital.

Heidi DeBoer updated her status.

June 04, 2016 – 5:41 p.m.

Going to stay home tonight; I feel very guilty not staying with him, but my back can't take sleeping in the pull out chair, and he isn't coming out of it—he is sleeping continuously. I'm comforting myself with all this … ugh!

2BeCourageous updated their status.

June 05, 2016 – 8:27 a.m.

I got up at 4:00 a.m. to let the dogs out and decided to stay up and go to the hospital. Not much change, he is opening his eyes and shakes like he is having a seizure; his tremors are in both hands and arms now. I said to him, "I love you," and he said 'okay' back. Then closed his eyes and was gone again. I need to be in both places at once tomorrow. Here when his doctor comes in, and Chessie wants me in the delivery room with her. What do I do? I want to be with Chessie really bad but afraid I will miss the doctor to see where we are at and what decisions must be made. Feeling very overwhelmed.

Jake, Chessie, and I had a long talk last night about Chet's wishes in his living health care paperwork. My kids are so strong and brave and have it together over all this. We made some decisions I couldn't do without their input and they made so much sense, way better than I was doing on my own. I will be going home to have lunch with Chesanne and her family and Jake. I'm so tired and I did sleep some. Then I will come back to Chet. Chessie goes into the hospital at midnight. My baby boy, Kyden Ander, will be here tomorrow! I can't wait to see him. Will he be another redhead? Or a blondie? Thanks for reading my stuff.

– Heidi

2BeCourageous updated their status.

June 05, 2016 – 5:16 p.m.

Well, after making decisions about Chet and considering palliative care, he ate parts of his three meals today; he is more awake and, when I told him I loved him, he said I love you back to me and wouldn't let go of my hand. So, now I am back at the struggle of what to do and how to proceed. My heart melted when he said I love you back, even though I'm not sure he knew me or not, it grabbed me. The stress is huge. I'm going to let them put him in rehab for physical therapy and assessment. Because of this wake up of his, it pretty much shows it was the Haldol that messed him up and I'm not sure he will fully recover to where he was.

Heidi DeBoer updated her status.
June 06, 2016 – 7:43 a.m.
The day has come! At the hospital with Chesanne, waiting for contractions to kick in good! So excited! Chet had a good night, tried to get out of bed twice but his body was against him, so he didn't get far. If I had thought this out, I would have put Chet in St. Thomas Murfreesboro where Chessie is having her baby instead of thirty some miles the other way.

2BeCourageous updated their status.
June 06, 2016 – 9:30 a.m.
At the hospital in Murfreesboro with my daughter who is in labor, and Chet is still in the hospital in Nashville doing better.

2BeCourageous updated their status.
June 06, 2016 – 11:54 a.m.
Just talked to the head of Palliative Care Team at Vanderbilt. Things are getting real now. They will decide his needs in the next couple days; he is not getting back to where he was and it's still a guessing game whether it is the Haldol or his Alzheimer's getting worse. Well, to me, it's obvious that the Haldol made his Alzheimer's worse and he isn't going to get back to where he was. She said she could see he isn't back to where he was and, if he stays this way, physical therapy will do no good and no point, which my friend who works in long-term care said too. So, palliative care means keeping him comfortable until he reaches the hospice stage, then let God take it from there. Oh, no baby yet; come on, Kyden!

Heidi DeBoer updated her status.
June 06, 2016 –8:21 p.m.

I had three to four phone calls today from different departments from Vanderbilt. They tracked me down at Chessie's hospital and home. One conversation, the lady, I think a social worker, said Chet was back at baseline, meaning like he was before the Haldol shut him down. She even said PT was in and I asked, "Did they get him up?" "Oh yes," she said. Well I get there late afternoon, and he is lying there full of poo and both arms shaking wildly out of control. His arms are so tight or stiff. No way he could walk like that. Baseline? I think not. There is no way he walked today or got up. He isn't even close to baseline except he is awake now. Frustrating.

2BeCourageous shared Heidi DeBoer's post.
June 06, 2016 – 8:28 p.m.

The newest member of the family, Kyden Ander Plung; eight pounds, a blondie, my daughter Chessie's beautiful son. He decided he didn't want to wait around and decided to speed up the labor process. He came fast! Feeling blessed to be there to witness his birth.

2BeCourageous updated their status.
June 07, 2016 – 1:36 p.m.

Been at the hospital with Chet since 6:30 a.m., now 1:30 p.m. Think I'm going home. Chet is very awake; he didn't sleep much at all in the night, they said. So, he is too awake and, when he does fall asleep now during the day, someone comes in and wakes him up; poor guy can't catch a break.

Palliative Care Team is going to assign me an outpatient palliative care team, so, even if we go to a nursing home short-term, I won't get lost in the shuffle. He will be coming home, but they want to see if they can bring some of what he lost this last week back as far as walking, etc. So, I've agreed on short-term only, not sure where yet. I just know he won't be there long because he isn't going to do what he is asked, he doesn't get most things, and, if he can't show improvement, the insurance will stop paying. But they want to try to see if he did lose skills from the Haldol or if it is his Alzheimer's turning worse. If it's the Alzheimer's, we take a different route and, if it's the drug, he will improve.

I think the drug did permanent damage and the neurologist said today that is why she doesn't do antipsychotics on dementia patients, and, if she does, it's not the ones he has been on. His PCP prescribed these and I still blame the neurologist because she blew us off onto the PCP who is not familiar with dementia that well by saying she is the one I should follow up with. I'm going home! I wouldn't trade his neurologist or his primary care doctor for a new one; they are great ladies.

Heidi DeBoer updated her status.
June 07, 2016 – 8:29 p.m.
I got to hold my new grandson for the first time today. Nothing like it! I'm beat, just tired, hoping Chessie and baby come home tomorrow. They are supposed to but Kyden has a bit of jaundice, so hoping his levels are good to go home tomorrow. Running between two counties to two hospitals can wear on a grammy! (Laughing)

Heidi DeBoer updated her status.
June 07, 2016 – 10:15 p.m.
Just to note, I have not had a pain pill since Monday night. Pain levels are really good, meaning hardly any sciatic pain in my leg for a week now! Praise God for that! Well, the surgeon to, I guess.

Heidi DeBoer updated her status.
June 09, 2016 – 1:29 p.m.
Well, they want to send Chet home; never got him up to walk or any PT to get him ready after being in bed for six days straight. They tried new drugs last night for the first time due to agitation. Guess what one it is? Seroquel, an antipsychotic! Really? Yes, he is hard to handle, and, yes, he was cussing and slapping the sitter's hand. But really? He wants out of there for sure. The only nursing home of the ones with closed/locked

units in the entire area is on the west end of Nashville, a thirty-five-minute drive with no one else on the road; morning and evening traffic, a good hour or more. I can't afford that every day. There was one that was an option yesterday, but not today that I'd consider in Murfreesboro. I'm so tired of always having to fight battles when it comes to our health!

2BeCourageous updated their status.
June 10, 2016 – 8:06 p.m.
After asking Jake to be honest about his wishes for his dad, he wants him home, I want him home, the doctor said he would do best at home, so he is coming home! Yes, I may complain about that decision once he is back, but Facebook is my release and helps me cope better, especially when I get good advice from y'all. So, let me complain and vent without hearing "I told you so" or you should have done this or that. We are doing what is best for all of us right now, and I have thirty days to put him in a home and insurance will still cover it after his hospitalization. So, that option is still on the table. Plus, he will get PT and OT at home from our health care agency and nurses coming in a couple of times a week. A palliative team member is going to call me today or Monday also.

2BeCourageous updated their status.
June 10, 2016 – 8:17 p.m.
We went and bought supplies to take care of Chet at home, then we went to pick him up and brought him home. He is a challenge right now because he can't walk without someone supporting him. Jake and I walk him wherever he thinks he wants to be instead of the wheelchair because his muscles need the workout. If only he would be happy in a spot for more than ten minutes.

I crushed his pills and got him butterscotch pudding, his favorite, to down them in. That went well. He is asleep right now in bed. He was so happy we came and got him. "Let's Go," he said. (Laughing) Thank you for the prayers, keep them coming to help us through this journey. God bless you all.

Heidi DeBoer updated her status.
June 10, 2016 – 10:26 p.m.
Chet slept very little in the hospital; his longest sound sleep was forty-five minutes straight. Otherwise, he would dose and wake up every ten to fifteen minutes and be agitated and restless. He has been sleeping for a couple of hours now and he wakes up startled, and I tell him he is home safe with Heidi, his wife, and Jake, his son, and he is in his own bed. He says, "Oh good," and fell back to sleep. Did this twice now. Sweetness arises within this dreaded disease.

2BeCourageous updated their status.
June 11, 2016 – 7:19 a.m.
Chet slept most of the night, his first best sleep since he was hospitalized, so that shows me being home is better since his longest straight sleep in the hospital was forty-five minutes straight. Our problem this morning is he seems to be in pain, and we are guessing bladder or kidney stone. We treated him for this, but we are guessing. He understands what we are saying to him; he seems better in that sense. I think his brain is telling him to move, move, move because he can't sit still.

Heidi DeBoer updated her status.
June 11, 2016 – 4:54 p.m.
Went to the doctor for Chet for a bladder or kidney infection. His back hurts in the kidney area, but he is not a willing to pee on command anymore so we couldn't test it. So, she prescribed an antibiotic to treat one just in case. He is very irritable and agitated and so is my son from lack of sleep. Ugh, all males in this house even the dogs. I'm outnumbered.

2BeCourageous updated their status.
June 12, 2016 – 2:13 p.m.
Does anyone else's spouse or loved one with dementia breathe heavy and fast just through their nose, with the mouth shut? I took him in last month for this and the primary care physician took blood tests to make sure he

isn't having problems with diabetes, and/or kidney that can cause carbon monoxide poisoning within his system that can be caused by those two things. Nothing came back positive. Then it stopped, but, since he has been home, he is doing it even worse. Didn't do it in the hospital, I think it may be a response to pain; he is being treated for bladder infection even though we couldn't get a urine sample to test.

2BeCourageous updated their status.
June 12, 2016 – 2:23 p.m.
Beware of giving your loved one with dementia certain antipsychotics, it put Chet in the hospital for seven days; his body reacted horribly to it. He couldn't walk, feed himself, he drooled, and so much more; he couldn't wake up. It says right in the warnings not to give to elderly dementia patients; he went on one coming off another, and he paced and paced and couldn't sleep and punched my son in the stomach on that one. He will not fully recover; it made his tremors worse also. Just a warning, though we can't prove it was the drug, we believe it was.

2BeCourageous added a new photo.
June 12, 2016 – 9:54 p.m.
He is so out of it today and paced the entire day; he is walking okay again now but ends up in weird positions when he crashes to sleep for five minutes at a time. We just decided not to ask anything of him and let him pace, not that we had a choice really. I'm sure it's the Seroquel. I hate these antipsychotics. I wish there were something to calm him with no side effects. His temper is high also. He doesn't want to eat, but I press the issue on that for now. He would walk circles in the living room and kitchen and stop for a bite to eat on his way past the table. At the doctor's, he was down to 153 pounds; last time we were there, I thought he was in the low 170s. Hard to believe he weighed over 260 once in his life. His legs are toothpicks now. Thanks for your prayers and support.

2BeCourageous updated their status.
June 12, 2016 – 10:06 p.m.

This coming week, we should be getting a routine down with the home nursing staff, plus they will do OT and PT evaluations and then come in one or two times a week. Also, the outpatient palliative care team is supposed to call me. Plus, the Humana Insurance case manager is supposed to come out once a week too. And we have another nurse that calls once or twice a month from Humana too. I like them for a Medicare Advantage plan. It's starting to sound busy and too many people, though we will see how it goes.

Heidi DeBoer updated her status.
June 14, 2016 – 8:18 a.m.

Not a happy camper, Chet continues to pace with very little breaks with the pacing to rest. The doctor is considering putting him back into the hospital because the two medications they changed him to can cause this. I hate psych drugs. I don't know how he is standing with little sleep! His doctor is on vacation. He slept restlessly from 10:00 p.m. to 1:30 a.m., he has been walking since; he sits down five minutes at a time maybe. That feeling must feel torturous, I've been on drugs that did that. I was on Seroquel for eight to nine years, though for sleep and didn't have side effects except for extreme hunger. Shows how different people react differently to the same drug.

2BeCourageous updated their status.
June 14, 2016 – 9:35 a.m.

Chet is going back to ER this morning; he can't stop himself from pacing and gets agitated.

2BeCourageous updated their status.
June 14, 2016 – 11:02 p.m.

So, okay, Jake and I just got home and I felt bad leaving Chet; he was still in ER, in an actual ER room and not a hallway, and he was knocked out because he was combative and being naughty. They are admitting him into the regular medicine hospital tonight, and he will remain there until the psych ward has an opening. No beds are available. There isn't a separate geriatric unit; it's part of the adult psych unit but they have a team of doctors who are geriatric specialists, I guess, that work with Alzheimer's patients like what Chet is going through. I really won't know what the heck it all is until he gets there. It's one psych ward I've managed to stay out of, so I'm not familiar with their set up.

I just find humor in the entire process. We get there and tell them his doctor is referring him to the psych ward for medication adjustments. Eight hours later, they tell us they think the psych ward is where he should be for medication adjustments. (Laughing)

While waiting to get into the ER floor, they had us sit away from the general public waiting room because Chet was acting out loudly. Two ladies came and sat by us. I told them he might start cussing any minute (so they won't be offended). The lady looks at me and laughs and says, "I might start cussing any minute too!" I laughed and said, "Oh, good, as long as we are all on the same page!" (Laughing out loud.)

If you don't find humor sitting for twelve hours in an ER with my husband who is strapped in a wheelchair and tries to walk away while still tied in it, one would go crazy or be arrested! Please pray they can find a medication for him that won't harm him but help him so we can manage him at home.

2BeCourageous updated their status.
June 15, 2016 – 9:21 p.m.
UPDATE: Chet has been transported tonight from Vanderbilt to a psych hospital in Murfreesboro. I went there before he got there and filled in the paperwork. He had a rough day and they kept him sedated with Ativan into his IV at Vandy. I feel I have no control now. Meaning, I need to be there to protect him, make sure he is being treated good, etc. I hate this! I have no say when I can see him. Visiting hours are three days a week for one hour. The average stay is three days to a week, but he said some

stay longer. The goal is to get Chet medicated, so he is comfortable and not being driven mad by the medications that are meant to help him, and not having these gosh-awful side effects that would make anyone crazy. If they can get him to the point where he is calm and can relax, then we can manage him at home. Please pray for this. I'm being given a God lesson in all this and I'm pouting!

2BeCourageous updated their status.
June 16, 2016 – 3:52 a.m.
At 3:49 a.m., I got a call from the psych hospital that Chet is on his way to St. Thomas ER. He tipped the wheelchair over on top of himself and had a bump on his head and a broken finger, they think! AHHHHHH! Left right away for the ER in Murfreesboro.

2BeCourageous commented on their post.
June 16, 2016 – 5:22 a.m.
UPDATE: I'm in St. Thomas ER in Murfreesboro with him. Huge egg-sized bump on his forehead and his pinky finger was dislocated, sticking out sideways. Doctor relocated it and just had an x-ray to see if it's broken; he needs CT scan of the head. Ugh! Not a great start to the new hospital he is in. What a difference in general hospitals from [being] overpacked at Vandy to no one here at St. Thomas. After they had cleared him, I had to take him back to the psych hospital. I felt so bad leaving him there.

2BeCourageous updated their status.
June 16, 2016 – 11:22 a.m.
Um … sigh, they just returned Chet to the ER in Murfreesboro for a concussion, having signs of sweating. (He has been sweating for a month, I told them that!) Confusion, um, he is on late-stage Alzheimer's, right? Oh my gosh, plus they drugged him out at the ER the first time with Ativan to do the CT scan. I'm suddenly not confident in the psych hospital right now. Why didn't they call me first? Now, I don't have the car, so I'm just going to wait for it then go down there. Sigh! No, I'm not stressed, I'm

losing my mind; maybe he and I can be roommates at the psych ward! He has been in three hospitals in a twenty-four-hour period; St Thomas is keeping him.

Heidi DeBoer updated her status.
June 16, 2016 – 3:50 p.m.
Ugh! What the heck! I'm so mad and upset. If Chet stays in the state he is in, the psych hospital can't keep him; he is too unmanageable for them. WHAT? You are a freaking psychiatric hospital! Hello? Oh my gosh! I'm losing it! The ER doctor just called and they will keep him overnight to try and break the agitation cycle he is in. I thought, *What about my agitation cycle?* Wonder if they can't break his? You do realize that a nursing home won't keep him either?! I know of dementia people kicked out of nursing homes due to their behavior! He is so agitated he swung at me in ER today. I'm just crying. They are going to try and fix him overnight at the general hospital, St. Thomas! I'm at a loss, all I have done is complain for days! There is nothing left to say to me, y'all are praying and loving me and I'm scared!

Heidi DeBoer updated her status.
June 16, 2016 – 8:34 p.m.
Can it get any more ridiculous? He had a second fall, thus a second CAT scan and an MRI in the same day. You all wonder why I don't want him in a facility. I called ER and they told me he was released against medical advice. What the heck? Blood pressure, check. I call the psych hospital, they tell me he is still at St. Thomas. My blood pressure is going higher. I call St. Thomas again and, oh yes, he is there in a room, but I'm not allowed information because I wasn't there on the second trip to ER because I don't have a special code! Now, you want to see a raving maniac lose it? Here I am! I crashed and slept this afternoon and dealt with this when I woke up. Jake is on his way home to go with me so I do not get arrested. We only have one car between us. Two falls and he is in good care!

Heidi DeBoer updated her status.
June 16, 2016 – 11:49 p.m.

My husband, he was the kindest, polite, godly man; a loving man who never—well, okay—hardly cussed and was such a blessing to all that knew him. He truly cared about others, loved to have company, and loved to cook. He was the best father I could have asked for our kids and such a wonderful husband to me. Always putting family first. Loved to laugh. Hated to lose. He was a hard worker. Though he is not dead and very much alive, I miss who he was and everything about him. The last week has been horrible and I ask myself how he would have handled this all. With class and kindness, he would have told me to turn to God, that He would help us. My husband wasn't perfect, but he was perfect for me! (Thinking about old memories with Chet DeBoer.)

Heidi DeBoer was feeling discouraged.
June 17, 2016 – 9:39 a.m.

The doctor came in, she insists he belongs in that psych hospital, where he fell in his wheelchair and broke his finger and smashed his head, for medication adjustments. "They have sent him out twice." I told her, "I would be surprised if they say yes. Plus, he won't wake up now!"

She blew off, "Where is the line?" Too difficult of a question, she says, so I will decide for all them. God help me! Someone visit me, I'm going nutso! HA!

2BeCourageous shared Heidi DeBoer's post.
June 17, 2016 – 8:59 a.m.

Sitting here alone with Chet in the hospital, listening to him breathe while he sleeps. He had a rough night.

Heidi DeBoer updated her status.
June 17, 2016 – 10:06 a.m.

He fell trying to get out of wheelchair at the psych hospital (I think) and has a broken finger; it was dislocated, not splinted; it was facing sideways but now fixed. They won't splint it because they say he will just take it off. Big bump on forehead and bruised knees. Also, have photos of his knees bruised and one at the medicine hospital, lying exposed with his door open, strapped to the bed, no covers on him, or no diaper either. My husband may be out of it but he deserves better than that; he deserves to have his dignity. I'm so sad over this. I made a complaint. Hospitals love me, I bet.

Heidi DeBoer updated her status.
June 17, 2016 – 11:23 a.m.
Chet's sister, Peg, in Michigan, her health is declining from her cancer and they have called in hospice. Please keep her and her family in prayer at this time!

Heidi DeBoer updated her status.
June 17, 2016 – 2:36 p.m.
If they think they are sending him back to the psych hospital when they had done nothing for him here except give him the same drug he was on at Vanderbilt, and he's in the same exact shape he was when he was at the psych hospital, this doctor is then mistaken. Do I have rights to not want him somewhere or will they write it up as against medical advice and then insurance won't pay?

Heidi DeBoer updated her status.
June 17, 2016 – 5:47 p.m.
My friend, Janita, from church bought Jake and I tickets to a benefit concert for the Bible Bowl kids trip. Several different singing and comedy groups there. Thought we would go; we never do anything. Looking forward to going. Thank you, Janita!

Heidi DeBoer updated her status.
June 17, 2016 – 11:32 p.m.
I came back to the hospital; I don't trust anyone with my husband now.

They were going to ship him back to the psych hospital he got hurt in, but one of the nurses stood up for me and said that I do not want him there while I was gone today. I'm not putting him in a place I cannot see him when I want.

Heidi DeBoer updated her status.
June 18, 2016 – 6:40 a.m.
Jake and I were treated by our friend, Janita, to a benefit concert last night at our church for the kids' Bible Bowl team. What great music and comedy, what a great group of people; we have not been in a while and we received such warm welcomes. I didn't even know that many of the folks read my stuff but knew what was going on. Did I say a great group of people? Yup! True story!

2BeCourageous updated their status.
June 18, 2016 – 10:34 a.m.
I talked to the doctor and talked her out of a psych hospital. I told her, "No psych hospital wipes butts and feeds the patient or takes 100% care. Plus, you are sending him to one exactly in the condition he was before, and they sent him back twice. They don't want him there." She told me I made sense. Yay! I make sense! (Laughing) So, I said to her, "I agree to the twenty days stay for rehab if it is in La Vergne, Smyrna, or Murfreesboro in a memory care unit." The caseworker is here today to work on it. They have not treated him here, they only have sedated him.

Heidi DeBoer updated her status.
June 18, 2016 – 12:09 p.m.
I'm in the room with Chet and I look away, and he has stripped down to nothing and pulled the IV out. So, after complaining of finding him that way alone the other night, I realized things happen, and I can't control the situation sitting twenty feet from him. My bad!

Heidi DeBoer updated her status.

June 18, 2016 – 5:11 p.m.

No change in Chet, but how could there be? All they do is sedate him with Ativan. Jake talked me into coming home; I spent the night last night there and all day today. Not sure what I will do tomorrow. Feeling down and tired.

Heidi DeBoer updated her status.

June 18, 2016 – 8:06 p.m.

I just picked up the remote and pointed it at the TV and pushed some buttons and it wouldn't work ... it was the house phone! (Laughing)

2BeCourageous updated their status.

June 19, 2016 – 12:32 a.m.

With Alzheimer's, as with any disease that brings loss of function and loss of life, there is a mourning process that goes with each piece lost. With Chet, I mourned and I still mourn for the pieces missing from himself. His humor, his wit, his eyes that said so much to me, and so on.

Mathew 5:4 NIV Bible says, "Blessed are they that mourn, for they will be comforted."

While I am mourning my husband who is still alive, I do not feel blessed nor do I feel comforted, though I know the process makes us stronger for going through it. I do not know what the verse means to God, all I can do is say we will see each other again, and Chet will be whole like he was and my comfort will come in seeing him again in Heaven.

Heidi DeBoer updated her status.

June 20, 2016 – 3:30 p.m.

I just love letters from the health insurance company denying his stay at Vanderbilt because his vitals were normal! You want to see one unpleasant lady right now, come on over! Unbelievable!

"A time to be born, and a time to die; a time to plant, and a time to pluck up what is planted."

ECCLESIASTES 3:2 ESV

CHAPTER 20

THE BEGINNING OF THE END (HOSPICE)

Heidi DeBoer updated her status.

June 21, 2016 – 9:36 a.m.

I talked to the doctor. I said, "I would like him to have PT and OT while he is here."

She said, "He can't, he is a fall risk and isn't capable of PT."

I said, "The case manager and yourself are trying to place him in rehab and insurance will not pay if he can't do anything."

She says, "Yes, that's right."

I said, "They won't take him, period! So, our only option's is to take him home."

She said, "We can't place him for rehab, the case manager sent out referrals for placement." (Am I the only one confused at this point?)

"For rehab?" I ask.

"Yes," she says. (Me laughing.)

"Why put him in a facility that he will get kicked out of? Let's bring him home; he can get PT there," I said.

She tells me, "If you want to take him home, we will arrange it."

So, I guess he is coming home, still out of it and she had no plan to help him, so we are going to follow Vandy's plan. I talked to head of palliative care, they will be coming out to take an assessment and he has a home health care team set up with, hopefully, respite set up also. We are putting him in Jake's room, his bed is lower and it's a straight shot with the wheelchair without rearranging my room. Jake will sleep in the den.

2BeCourageous updated their status.

June 22, 2016 – 3:01 a.m.

Chet has been approved for hospice. They will take over any medical appointments and needs and they will come to him. They will make sure he isn't in pain and always comfortable as can be. They told me it doesn't mean death is in the very near future; they have had patients on hospice up to two years. I do not wish that, though, for my husband, a two-year hospice; he has no quality of life as it is. I am not sure what to expect until it all happens.

Today, he is in the hospital waiting on discharge. All they did for him was sedate him the entire time. Hospice said, if we want to take Chet out on an outing, we can, there are no restrictions on him. I'm not sure he will be well enough to go out again, but it's an option he can do if he is feeling up to it. As far as respite, we get five days every ninety days and volunteers come for short times away, like going to a movie, etc. for Jake and I, and they will watch Chet. I think we will all start to feel a little better with this organization taking over. I prayed and told his neurologist I need someone to be in charge and make decisions about his care, well, hospice showed up from the same home health agency we already belong to. Thank you, God!

2BeCourageous updated their status.
June 22, 2016 – 3:07 a.m.
Jake's room is set up for Chet—hospital bed, oxygen tanks, fancy air mattress, and some machine I have no idea about. Chet got here around 8:00 p.m. The hospice nurse is coming out in a few. Not to stay, just to do orientation type stuff.

2BeCourageous updated their status.
June 22, 2016 – 3:08 a.m.
The day has been kind of stressful, just like the last twenty.

I did well with the hospice people and letting it soak in, up until I was to choose a funeral home. Then I froze and had enough. She said I could research them if I wanted. So, I will look around. Lying in bed, not feeling well physically, and part of it is my ulcers acting up, and I won't mention I hurt my back, pulling Chet up in bed with Jake. So, yeah, I know you all told me so, but I don't have a choice; I have to move him, hoping there is an easy way that someone will show me because this is going to suck if there isn't.

Heidi DeBoer updated her status.
June 23, 2016 – 9:00 a.m.
So far, on this journey of six years, mourning each loss Chet has gone through, God gave us new life to hold onto and cherish and make the lows seem less low. Newborn life twice and what a blessing they are to our family. Loving on Braydon Michael and Kyden Ander.

2BeCourageous shared Heidi DeBoer's post.
June 23, 2016 – 8:26 p.m.
Chet is on hospice care at home, we have been told to make final arrangements even though him dying isn't immediate; hospice is guessing three to six months. Something I know is coming but wasn't ready to run out and do. A chaplain was here today and brought it up again, saying it will

be easier now to do then after he passes. He said he would go with me if I wanted him too. Early-onset Alzheimer's, I hate you!

2BeCourageous shared Heidi DeBoer's post.
June 27, 2016 – 5:03 p.m.
Got Chet up in the wheelchair for a shave and cleaning of the beard. He is watching TV with his eyes closed but says he doesn't want to go to bed. Hospice comes mainly on Tuesdays and Thursdays with an RN, and a nurse aide comes to wash him or shower him. The aide, we can get three days if we need her. Chaplain comes twice a month or more if needed, social worker once or twice a month. Not sure when the nurse practitioner comes. Waiting for the respite coordinator to call.

2BeCourageous updated their status.
June 28, 2016 – 11:56 a.m.
Rough start to the day, kind of like road rage only [it's] caregiver rage; just mad for no reason and cussing like a sailor. Not reflecting Christ very well right now. Even the dogs hid. I'm not perfect, I'm not a saint, I'm not a hero. I get angry and can't give you a reason, just overwhelmed and so tired of washing sheets four times a day because either the cheap hospice diapers leak every time, or he is deliberately peeing everywhere but in the diaper. Going to have to buy the Depend for men again; we never had this problem before wetting the bed every time he pees. Vent, vent, vent, I am me and nothing special; I am me and I'm mad today. I am me!

2BeCourageous updated their status.
June 30, 2016 – 5:29 p.m.
Oh, my word, Jake and Chessie were leaving to get my birthday dinner to bring back to me and Jake came back in the house, he forgot his wallet. Chet just climbed over the hospital bed railing and crashed into the wheelchair next to the bed. Hit his head and leg and shoulder are scraped up. Thank God Jake was here to help Chet and me. He is back in bed; I called hospice to find out what to do. They told me to give him extra meds

of this and that, so I did. Dear Lord, keep this man in bed and clothed! I can't protect him at home any better than the hospital did. If he is determined to get up, he will do it even if he hurts himself.

Heidi DeBoer updated her status.
July 01, 2016 – 4:29 a.m.
Can it get any worse? Hush, it can but I just want to scream or cry right now. Husband won't leave the diaper on and messes the sheets, and Robb, at 3:00 am, got sprayed directly onto the face by a skunk again! Jake is out buying more tomato juice as I'm outside washing him! How do you get rid of a skunk? I would buy a gun right now if I could shoot the thing in the city! It gets in our fence and we can't see where!

Heidi DeBoer updated her status.
July 01, 2016 – 3:57 p.m.
I bet y'all are wondering what else could go wrong in our lives here, right? Well, let me tell ya. I was in the shed cleaning and came out and down the steps and rolled the ankle that I broke three years ago in a freshly dug hole at the bottom of the step during the time inside the shed. Yes, Robb! My skunk dog!

Debating to get an x-ray; I have a plate and pins on one side and screw on the other side of the ankle. But the surgeon told me three years ago I could very easily break it again. I called my ninety-two-year-old mommy and cried to her. I want my mommy! (Laughing) No, really!

Heidi DeBoer updated her status.
July 01, 2016 – 6:01 p.m.
Got several x-rays and, because of the old scar tissue and breaks, they need a CAT scan. The pain is on the top of the foot and swollen there. The ankle feels fine, and the hardware doesn't look damaged. She said where she thinks I should be hurting, I'm not. Hmmm. So, I have to wear a boot until I get a CAT scan end of next week if it's still bad by then.

2BeCourageous updated their status.
July 04, 2016 – 7:20 p.m.
I'm not sure what to write, I have mixed feelings about hospice. They are great, kind, caring, and will come out at any given moment if needed. I can call any time of the night and day with concerns. But the one concern they can't help me with is the concern or the feeling that I'm aiding in his death. I talked to a mom whose twenty-three-year-old son was in hospice with Lewy body dementia over a year ago. She said she felt the same way, the same thing. I feel like I'm killing him by standing by and doing nothing to save him. I'm Doctor Mom, he used to call me. But I can't make him better. I know he is dying and I knew he would die from this disease the entire time. I've not fooled myself into believing otherwise, but, here we are, and I feel totally helpless. I'm not sure that the pain medication, morphine, I give him is really for pain anymore, but to advance the process instead. They don't say that but I'm also not stupid. So, I feel like I have a hand in the dying process and God knows he doesn't want to live like he has been, and God knows he wants to be in Heaven; I just wish God would take over now and take him and not prolong his suffering anymore. God didn't cause this disease in him, but He can take him when He chooses.

Heidi DeBoer updated her status.
July 06, 2016 – 12:10 a.m.
I laid down to take a nap yesterday, and I wake up to Chessie and baby sleeping on the couch and Jake sleeping in the den and Chet sleeping and Braydon, four, lying on the other couch, playing video games on his mom's phone. Laughing … sleepy household that left the four-year-old in charge, I guess.

2BeCourageous updated their status.
July 06, 2016 – 8:32 p.m.
Sometimes, Chet's and my eyes will meet, and that does not happen hardly at all anymore that he will make eye contact with me, but, when they do

meet, I feel and see his disdain for what is happening to him. The endless pool of love his eyes used to give out, I can't see. All I can say to him is, "I love you and I'm so sorry you are on this road, but I promise it will lead to Heaven and you will be well again." Then I must stop and wonder what he sees in my eyes if anything.

2BeCourageous updated their status.
July 08, 2016 – 1:31 a.m.

My sister-in-law, Peggy (Chet's oldest sister), passed away in the early morning hours of July 7th yesterday. She fought a long, hard battle with brain tumors. She was an amazing lady and so fun to be around. I loved her laugh. It breaks my heart that we can't go to Michigan for the celebration of her life. I told Chet about his sister's passing. He can't talk anymore but made a groaning noise that sounded like a sound of despair. I told him she was well again in Heaven and with his mom and dad.

The tension was high in the house yesterday and my son and I had words; he came to me to apologize and, as he talked, he said that, with his Aunt Peg's passing, it all became so real to him about his dad. Yes, he accepts and knows his dad is dying, but, at the same time, he said he doesn't want to lose his dad. The permanence of that thought, I think, was weighing on us all today. We can say we accept what's to come, then, like yesterday, the reality of it comes with a phone call that one of our precious lives has ended here on earth.

Losing Peg was huge for our family, gatherings won't be the same, the six siblings are now five soon to be four, but, for those of us still waiting for our time, life has to go on for the living. Yes, we must mourn, it's only natural to feel loss and hurt, and that's okay. For those that pass ahead of us, we are still living and we will again be together, never to be separated again by life and death for we will all have an eternal life together. This is what gets us through, the memories and the knowing that Jesus made it possible for us to have eternity with all our loved ones that accepted Him as their savior. Carrying on and living life is 2BeCourageous. Peggy, we will miss you terribly, but we are very happy for your new life in Heaven.

2BeCourageous updated their status.

July 08, 2016 – 7:17 a.m.

Chet is having a bad morning congestive-wise in his throat, I'm assuming in his chest too but have no idea until the nurse gets here from hospice. They had me give him two doses of atropine drops, which quieted it down. I started shaking this morning listening to him, so I got Jake up for a bit so I wasn't alone until Chet calmed down with his congestion. Some call it the death gurgle. Dear Lord, help me be strong.

Heidi DeBoer updated her status.

July 08, 2016 – 10:52 a.m.

Well, hospice was just here; congestion is not in his lungs yet, but they are going from twice a week to everyday visits of the nurse. No more medications crushed up that he has to eat due to choking hazard and aspiration into his lungs. Even stopping his diabetes medication since feeding has been stopped. He was storing the food in his cheeks and not swallowing much of it. He is forgetting or has forgotten how to swallow. Only morphine and atropine to break up the congestion in his throat, or as it says on the bottle for terminal secretions. He is calm, with oxygen good, blood pressure good, so far, lungs okay. Now, for me to digest all the things we are stopping and to not play head games with myself. Thank you in advance, prayer warriors, that God be kind and swift.

2BeCourageous shared Heidi DeBoer's post.

July 08, 2016 – 10:53 a.m.

Pray for God's mercy on my husband. After telling him about Peg, I told Chet that Peggy was waiting for him at the gates of Heaven and that it's okay to go meet her and walk through together. I asked him if he could hear me. He said weakly, "Yes."

2BeCourageous updated their status.

July 09, 2016 – 3:35 p.m.

I woke up mid-morning, sleeping longer than I wanted too. I jumped out of bed and went right to Chet's room. He was lying there and wouldn't respond to me when I talked to him; I felt him and he was warm and, for some reason, I lifted his hand and it was warm and limp. He was nonresponsive. I went and took a shower for hospice was due to come soon. After I got dressed and took care of the dogs, I went back in to sit with Chet and started talking to him. I felt his head while I was telling him I loved him. It was cold! I yelled his name with no response whatsoever. I grabbed his hand and lifted his arm, he was cold and stiff. I ran and got Jake up and cried, "I think Daddy died!" He hurried into the room. He felt him too, and he felt for a pulse. My love of my life was gone. Hospice got there shortly after, and I fell apart when she announced him dead.

Chester Dale DeBoer passed away this morning, July 9th, 2016. I believe he met his sister at the gates of Heaven and they walked through together. He no longer suffers from this dreaded disease. He is now free, free from the pain and torture. He is whole again in Heaven and happy with family that had passed before us. While I rejoice that he is well again, my heart is torn and I cannot hold the emotion back Oh God, why?!

"So with you: Now is your time of grief, but I will see you again, and you will rejoice, and no one will take away your joy."

JOHN 16:22 NIV

"Fear not, for I am with you; be not dismayed, for I am your God;
I will strengthen you, I will help you, I will uphold you with My
righteous right hand."

ISAIAH 41:10 NKJV

CHAPTER 21

MOURNING HAS BROKEN

Heidi DeBoer updated her status.

July 15, 2016 – 6:05 p.m.

The family is pulling in from Michigan; we are going to eat with Chet's brothers and sisters and nieces and nephews. Tomorrow is the celebration of life service for Chet DeBoer. Twenty-three family members here together; it's sad it couldn't be under other circumstances. So happy they are here, though!

2BeCourageous updated their status.

July 16, 2016 – 4:07 a.m.

I didn't just lose my husband with Alzheimer's; I lost my best friend, my lover, a gentleman, a godly man, a wonderful father, a great brother and uncle, and a good friend to others. I lost those dreamy eyes, the smile that lit my life. I lost the one person that knew me inside and out; I lost a man full of compassion and dreams. I lost my rock and my world.

God knew I would have trouble with this, so he gave me five plus years to practice being in charge. He gave me time to let it sink in, to show myself I can do it alone without my husband. Well, God, it wasn't enough time for me, but, at the same time, it went on too long for my husband, and now you have him in Heaven. So, please cherish all his special qualities and tell him he is missed by so many, and that we are so happy he is pain-free from this horrid disease and the world we live in and, especially, God, please tell him I will always love him, forever.

Heidi DeBoer updated her status.
July 16, 2016 – 5:10 p.m.
What a wonderful service for my husband and a wonderful turn out for him and us. Thank you to all that came and thank you to Michael and Amy for singing the song I chose! Thank you to Melissa for singing the song she chose, it was just beautiful, I loved it, and thank you to Pastor Randy for a great service and sermon and the ladies of Lakeshore Christian Church for the great food! And Greg for putting together the slide show and music! You all rock and I know Chet was so happy watching all of this.

Heidi DeBoer updated her status.
July 16, 2016 – 11:58 p.m.
Chet's wedding cowboy hat and boots and eagle urn and American Indian drum were all displayed in front of the church.

Eagles had a special meaning to Chet. The painting of the eagle flying was done by my daughter, Chesanne Plung, for her dad's memorial service. We set up Chet's favorite Western things, even his spurs, and the eagle statue we got him is his urn for his ashes and had the Bible verse put on it from Isaiah 40:31 NIV, [which] says ... "But those who hope in the LORD will renew their strength. They will soar on wings like eagles."

Heidi DeBoer updated her status.
July 17, 2016 – 5:02 a.m.

The easy way to cope with anger and hurt is to blame God. When, in reality, God doesn't do things to hurt us. But we assume He causes everything that hurts us, like Alzheimer's for instance. A God that is love wouldn't do that. He hates to see us suffer. But things of this world do cause us to hurt and to be angry. The devil is also a factor. But no one blames him for things. God will bring us through our trials, and He won't let us suffer more than we can handle. I believe He swooped my husband up and gave him rest and comfort and a new life in Heaven so that he would no longer suffer! That is an amazing, God! Yeah, I'm left behind with raw feelings but look at the hope I have in such a wonderful God. I know where I'm going when my time comes and how wonderful to have that to hang on to!

Heidi DeBoer updated her status.
July 18, 2016 – 12:24 a.m.

Jake took me bowling with Chessie, Brandon, Braydon, Jeremy, and Nick. I bowled one game and enjoyed it, then watched. Guilt took over, no need to lecture; I'm going to go through unreasonable emotions, so bring them on so I can get past them!

2BeCourageous updated their status.
July 19, 2016 – 6:23 p.m.

The last few days, I either sleep or stay busy during the day, but the silence of the night comes crawling in, and I go to a whole new level of despair because I'm not thinking of the man he was when he left; I'm thinking of the man he was before he got sick. I just miss him, our happily ever after here together was ruined, and he got his heavenly happily ever after already … you don't need the rapture to feel left behind.

Today is the twins' twenty-second birthday. Our twenty-fifth anniversary is tomorrow, the 20th of 2016.

Heidi DeBoer updated her status.
July 21, 2016 – 5:30 p.m.
Got a lot done today, went to the cremation center and filled out paperwork and submitted the life insurance paperwork, they did it for me. They gave us Chet's ashes. Also went to Social Security and waited what seemed an eternity to file for spouse benefits, so I will get Chet's instead of mine. Then wandered through Sam's Club, window shopping. Then home.

Heidi DeBoer updated her status.
July 21, 2016 – 5:34 p.m.
I've wanted wind chimes forever, so, when we got home today, there was a package in the door from Adoration Hospice. A beautiful wind chime with a bow around it. I couldn't have been more pleased!

Heidi DeBoer updated her status.
July 23, 2016 – 10:19 p.m.
We were very blessed the last two weeks to have Jake's good friend, Jeremy, home from the Navy and stay with us at our house. It's always a pleasure and made this hard time a bit easier on us by having the company. Missing him as he is back in Virginia, waiting to be called out on the ship in the next few months. Won't see him for a while. Hugs and love, Jeremy.

Heidi DeBoer updated her status.
July 24, 2016 – 1:55 p.m.
Went back to church at Lakeshore Christian Church for the first time since Chet got homebound, but the ole devil had that steering wheel and kept trying to get me to turn around and go home. God won, love wins.

Heidi DeBoer updated her status.
July 25, 2016 – 9:29 p.m.
Well, I successfully have weaned myself off hydrocodone, the pain med I've been on since November. The pain is pretty much gone from

sciatica down the back into the leg, which made life unbearable, so the surgery was a success. Second day on nothing at all. No bad withdrawals by weaning off them very slowly, cutting doses down and down over the last month. Now, to conquer the fibromyalgia pain. Oh, how I wish a surgery could cure that! Going to start working out but can't lift heavy weights, so I don't inflame the back, or I will bring it all back on me. I thought the pain would be there forever; thank you, Jesus, for answered prayer.

2BeCourageous updated their status.
August 04, 2016 – 11:00 p.m.
I've been keeping busy with my kids and even paid off some debt; I laugh and joke, well, because I'm just funny, I have to laugh at myself a lot. But, at the same time, I'm so sad and I can feel the depression creeping through my brain, so I'm on guard. I have suffered tremendous depression in my past with those big ups and desperate downs; I'm no stranger to it, so I know when it's creeping and sneaking in. I've stood against it for a long time, caring for my husband; he needed me. Now, "the void" has started and I know how fragile I feel at times, or Satan wants me to believe I am, looking for the opportunity to bring me down, but I need to keep my eyes on God. My strength comes from Him. There is just a piece of me gone, and I don't think that piece will ever come back. So, I need to fill in the gap and that's where God comes into this. He fills me with His love and that's what I will hold on to.

2BeCourageous updated their status.
August 15, 2016 – 12:12 a.m.
I managed to open Chet's side of the closet today and pack his clothes up. Not a fun job.

2BeCourageous updated their status.
September 06, 2016 – 10:14 a.m.

Today I looked for you, but didn't know where to start;
I finally found you tucked away in my heart.
Even though I hold you close to me and dear,
I miss you terribly as if you weren't near.
I'm waiting for you to come to me, in revealing dreams,
To make it all okay again and not a nightmare as this seems.
I wait for the day to see you, just once more,
But until that time comes, my heart shall remain tore.
I love and miss you.

by Heidi at 2BeCourageous

2BeCourageous shared Heidi DeBoer's post.
September 12, 2016 – 5:46 p.m.
Grocery shopping today, I found myself picking out stuff Chet liked; I looked at several items thinking I should get it but then didn't. Funny how the mind can mess with you.

2BeCourageous updated their status.
September 19, 2016 – 11:07 p.m.
It breaks my heart to read about others going through the dementia journey and all the same struggles we went through, knowing there is no cure or help to hold it off. Reading about people with dementia, and how their own family won't see them and back away from the person probably because they can't cope with it, is the saddest thing ever. We were so blessed to have both of our children right by our side, my son choosing to live with us to care for his dad and do online college instead of leaving for college. My daughter is coming over five to six hours a day most weekdays to be with us. We did have people in our lives stop visiting and calling and, believe me, it was hurtful. All you can do is give them a second chance, Christ would. Forgive them, Christ would. They probably don't

even realize they did something to hurt you. Everyone copes different with these diseases, don't hold on to hurt feelings. Life is so much better when you don't. Please, if you know someone with any type of dementia, don't be scared, don't back away; it could get to the point where they don't seem to know you, but you will always know them. Be there for them.

– Heidi at 2BeCourageous

2BeCourageous shared Heidi DeBoer's post.
September 24, 2016 – 12:22 a.m.
I read posts every single day where someone has died from a dementia disease. One person today said it well by saying their loved one was now *free*. I said that about Chet also. Free of this horrible disease that is taking younger and younger people every day. Free of the chains of these diseases. Chet is free and well again and knowing that makes my heart happy, and yet I'm still sad too, not having him here with me. I just miss that man so much, but I know we will be together again someday.

2BeCourageous shared Heidi DeBoer's post.
October 15, 2016 – 1:55 p.m.
This disease is going to hit someone you know in the next several years; don't let them walk it alone, don't let the caregiver walk it alone either; it's a very lonely journey.

2BeCourageous updated their status.
November 08, 2016 – 10:42 p.m.
I feel like a stranger in my own skin. On unfamiliar ground, lost in what direction to turn, so I stay put. I'm not so sure if I have a very good relationship with God. Not like I see others and their commitments. I wander around in my mind avoiding Him and finding myself convincing others, but mostly myself, that I am not mad at God. I'm not mad at Him! Or am I? I didn't think I was. I know He didn't plan my husband's illness, but, at the same time, He chose not to make him well here on earth. I try

and pray and talk to God daily but my mind wanders and I get lost in my thoughts, and God gets put on the back burner. I feel numb and I suppose this is all part of grieving. If I were mad at God, I suppose it would be normal considering ... but then I should be stronger than that, right?

One thing I have learned about grief is that it's normal. The crying, the bitterness and anger, the sadness, the emptiness, even being mad at God, it's all because we love that person we lost so much. It's love! There is no time limit on grief; grief lasts forever, what changes is the way we handle it. It becomes easier over time and we learn to smile when we talk about our loved ones. Our hearts feel less and less hurt and more of the love pours through, and we go on with our lives.

God gave the greatest gift in Chet DeBoer. I was honored to be his wife and he touched my life in a way that changed me for the better. He taught me how to pray to God freely, and he was my shining light. Dear Jesus, thank you for the time I had him; I will be forever grateful.

How my family and I chose to keep Chet home no matter what is not for everybody. Not everyone can do that. People work and, if you have no one to care for the loved one while you are working, you have to put them in a long-term care facility. If caregivers have no help at home, there comes the point where you have to put them in a home for your own sanity.

If I didn't have the help I did, I couldn't have managed to care for my husband near the end. I could promise him to keep him home because I knew I had the help. But, as you saw, it got to the point where we were ready to place him and everything kept going against it happening. For us, I believe God wanted him with us. We all wanted that. That is not for everyone. I stress this because I know how guilty caregivers get when they place a loved one in a facility. I get that. Just having Chet in the hospitals he was in, I felt some of that guilt.

Don't ever feel bad for making decisions that include what's good for you too. Caregivers need to take care of themselves. Being a caregiver is hard. It's the hardest thing I've ever done. Please don't beat yourselves up when you feel like quitting, look for respite care. If your loved one is in late stages, call for a hospice evaluation. They are a huge help, and your loved one doesn't need to be at the end of life to go on hospice. Here in Tennessee, we used Adoration Hospice. Best people ever!

Number one thing to get you through, coming from a Christian, is to stay focused on God. Go to Him daily, when things are good and when things are going bad. He is hope and love, and LOVE WINS!

MOURNING HAS BROKEN

I mourned you every day for the past six years,
and when I woke that one morning I knew time was very near.
But I didn't know you would leave me unannounced and slip away;
I always thought we would have at least one more day.
When I walked into the room that morning, my heart sank and died,
All the preparing I did, I wasn't prepared inside.
This mourning and hurt have no compare, to that of those past,
I want to scream your name to Heaven, all my anger I want to cast!
But I lay here silent with tears streaming down my face,
never feeling such an ache, feeling so out of place.
Sure, you are in a better place and whole again as we prayed,
You went on without me, and here I stayed.
Mourning has broken or is it just I?
My heart breaks for you; I feel I could die.
But, no, I will carry on amongst the grief and all the pain,
I'll make you proud, and I will continue to dance in the rain.

HEIDI DEBOER 2BECOURAGEOUS 8/2016 ©

Fast forward to 2019. Chessie is expecting a girl end of March. Answered prayer.

Braydon is seven and in first grade. I wrote a children's book about him that explains dementia to children called *Braydon the Red* on Amazon.

Jake graduated from Academy of Art University as a Director in Motion Pictures and Television.

Me … I can smile because I know I will see Chet again in Heaven and there is nothing better than that.

Figure 2 Chet and Heidi's engagement photo.

Figure 3 Chet and Heidi, July 20th, 1991.

Figure 4 Jake and Chessie at nine months old.

Figure 5 Chet, Heidi, Jake, and Chessie.

Figure 6 Heidi and Chet and Maggie

Figure 7 Jake and Chet and Maggie

Figure 8 Brandon and Chessie. Chet giving the bride away.

Figure 9 Chet and Heidi in the rain.

Figure 10 Jake and Chessie, April 12th, 2014.

Figure 11 Brandon, Chessie, and Braydon.

Figure 12 Chet with Chessie, wedding.

Figure 13 Robb

Figure 14 Chessie, Brandon, Braydon, Jake, Snow, Heidi, and Chet.

Figure 15 Jake and Heidi

Figure 16 Brandon, Chesanne, Braydon, and Kyden.

Figure 17 Painting Chesanne Plung did for the funeral.

Figure 18 Chet and Braydon

Figure 19 Chet DeBoer

Facebook Dementia Support Groups and Other Online Resources

Alzheimer's Association

www.alz.org

Dave Ramsey (website for legal papers)

www.daveramsey.com

Dementia Aware (UK)

https://www.facebook.com/groups/250325295027020/

Early Onset Alzheimer's Support Group

https://www.facebook.com/groups/220603604654873/

Forget Me Not

https://www.facebook.com/groups/
ForgetMeNotDementiaSupport/

Frontotemporal Dementia Support and Info

https://www.facebook.com/groups/ftdinfoandsupport/

Lewy Body Dementia Carers

https://www.facebook.com/groups/lyndseywilliams/

Vascular Dementia

https://www.facebook.com/groups/142489242562155/
?hc_ref=SEARCH

Feel free to private message Heidi DeBoer on Facebook:

https://www.facebook.com/hisyd https://www.facebook.
com/2BeCourageousHeidi/?ref=aymt_homepage_panel

About the Author

Heidi DeBoer, a Christian author, was born and raised in Grand Rapids, Michigan. She moved to Nashville, Tennessee area in 2006 with her family and has remained there with her adult children and grandchildren.

She has written *2BeCourageous (Living with a Stranger)* journaling her husband's early-onset Alzheimer's and FTD in hopes of helping caregivers feel less alone in their own journeys with these diseases. Heidi says it can get very disheartening and lonely on the journey. She shares how God has touched their lives many times and lists encouraging Bible verses to help give hope and understanding.

Heidi has also written a children's book called *Braydon the Red*, which is about a young boy learning that his grandpa has dementia, explaining in such a way to help the young minds understand the illness.

CPSIA information can be obtained
at www.ICGtesting.com
Printed in the USA
LVHW090247230819
628530LV00001B/4/P